COOL SCIENCE EXPERIMENTS

Published by Hinkler Books Pty Ltd 2015
45–55 Fairchild Street
Heatherton Victoria 3202 Australia
hinkler www.hinkler.com.au

© Hinkler Books Pty Ltd 2004, 2013, 2015

Illustrated by Glen Singleton
Cover design by Hinkler Books Design Studio
Cover illustration by Rob Kiely
Typeset by MPS Limited

ISBN: 978 1 4889 2621 1

Printed and bound in China

COOL SCIENCE EXPERIMENTS

Contents

Introduction

This book is full of simple science experiments to shock and amaze you. Ordinary materials like vinegar, string, eggs, and paper are used to make extraordinary things. They will help you find how science works, and why things happen the way they do. Most of all, these experiments are fun!

You will end up growing your own stalactites and be able to bounce an egg. Why not make a mobile out of gelatin, or cook up some home-made boogers? Your kitchen will never be the same when you create your own underwater volcano.

You will find most of the equipment you need for the experiments around the house. A good tip is to find an empty box and keep it stocked with things you might need. Don't throw out used jars, corks, or lengths of string. Why not store them in the box all ready for when you do your next experiment.

Acknowledgements

The experiments were tried, tested, and improved by the following very giggly children during their holidays and weekends – they had loads of fun. We hope you do too! ☆ Rebecca Chapman, ☆ Olivia Kenyon, ☆ Shivani Goldie, ☆ Katherine Jenkins, and ☆ Verity Maton.

A special thanks to the following big people too! ☆ Dr. Greg Chapman, ☆ Dr. Kate Kenyon, ☆ Lois Goldthwaite, ☆ Dr. Paul Maton, and ☆ Ann Jenkins.

Helen Chapman

Experiment Rating

Easy:	Medium:	Difficult:	Adult needed:
			+ 

Wait and See

1 The Bouncin' Egg

Rat's Rating

That's the first time I've ever seen an egg ride a pogo stick!

Anything's possible in Science I suppose!

Can an egg bounce without breaking? Wait! Don't try it yet. Read what to do first.

You will need:

eggs, water, vinegar, flashlight, bowl ☆

Rat's Helpful Hint

Don't do this experiment in a hot bath. The eggs will cook and get hard-boiled. Also, don't try this at the end of the week—eggs hate Fry-days.

For this biology experiment

1 Put 1 whole raw egg in a glass of water.

2 Put 1 whole raw egg in a glass of vinegar.

3 The eggs are the same, aren't they? Now, leave them for a few hours.

4 Look at both eggs. Do they still look the same? The egg in the water is the same, but the egg in the vinegar has changed. The shell has begun to fizz. The acid in the vinegar dissolves the calcium carbonate that's in the shell.

5 Look carefully. Does the egg in vinegar still have its shell? Touch it. It now feels and looks like a rubber ball, doesn't it?

Hey! Go easy!

☆ ☆ COOL SCIENCE EXPERIMENTS

6 Leave both eggs alone for 7 days. After that time, take the egg in vinegar to a dark room and shine a flashlight at it. What do you see? The light bounces off the egg, doesn't it?

7 Take the egg out of the glass of vinegar. Hold the egg a little bit over a bowl.

8 Let the egg drop. Do you think it will splatter? Try it!

What Happens

Your egg bounces! Try it again getting a little higher each time. See how high you can make the egg bounce. What do you think will happen if you try to bounce the egg that was in the water? Hold it over the bowl and try.

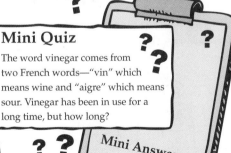

Why

- A chemical change takes place in the egg when left in vinegar.
- The vinegar, which is an acid, reacts with the calcium carbonate of the eggshell.
- The change makes the shell go soft, then disappear. This is called "decalcification".
- The egg in the glass of water does not chemically change.

Fun Fact

You can make chicken bones so soft that you can bend them. Put a clean wishbone or leg bone into a jar of vinegar. Make sure the bones are completely covered. Leave them there for 7 days. The bones will go so soft that you can twist them into a knot! Minerals in the bone make it strong and rigid. The vinegar takes away these minerals and the bones dissolve like the eggshell.

Just look at those legs! She's been soaking them in VINEGAR... You can tell!

Mini Quiz

The word vinegar comes from two French words—"vin" which means wine and "aigre" which means sour. Vinegar has been in use for a long time, but how long?

Mini Answer ✓
It is known that vinegar was used in Babylon in 5,000 B.C.

Grow a Stalactite

2

How long have you two been doing this?

Oh.... Only a couple of thousand years... But we're having a great time!

Have you ever been in a cave and seen amazing columns? These are "stalactites" and "stalagmites." It takes many hundreds of years for these to grow. You can make your own in just a few weeks!

Rat's Helpful Hint
If you get a chance to visit a dark cave, remember to hide around a corner. When someone passes by, leap out and shout "Boo! Adults just love this!

You will need:
glass jars, baking soda or Epsom salts (The salts take longer, but give you more shapes.), spoon, wool/cotton/string (any thread that will soak up water), paperclips, water, saucer

What to do for this chemistry experiment

1 Fill two clean jars with hot water.

2 Add as much baking soda to each jar as will dissolve.

3 Mix well so that the soda is dissolved completely.

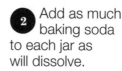

4 Dip each end of the thread into the jars. The ends must be weighed down with paperclips, pencils, popsicle sticks, or nails to keep them in the jars.

5 Place a saucer between the jars to catch the drips.

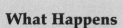

6 Let the thread hang between the jars and over the saucer.

7 Leave the jars for 2–3 weeks. Will anything grow?

What Happens

A white stalactite grows down from the wool and a stalagmite grows up from the saucer.

Why

- The baking soda mix is carried up through the thread. This is called *capillary action*.
- The mix then drips onto the saucer.
- Over the days, the dripping water evaporates. It leaves a little of the baking soda behind.
- These bits of baking soda make a tiny stalactite and stalagmite.
- After months, these join. They make a single column like the one you see in a cave.

Fun Fact

? ?

One of the world's tallest stalagmites is in Slovakia. Cavers found the 106.9 feet (32.6 meters) tall stalagmite in 1964.

DANGEROUS!

WHAT'S THE VIEW LIKE FROM UP THERE?

Mini Quiz **?**

What is the difference between stalactites and stalagmites?

? ?
?

Mini Answer ✓

Stalactites are the long rock columns that grow from the roof of a cave and hang down. Stalagmites look the same but they grow on the bottom of a cave and grow upward. When they meet, they make a column. They come from deposits of the mineral calcium carbonate in water that drips into the cave. To remember the difference between the two, think of this: stalactites hold tight ('tite') to the roof of the cave and stalagmites might (mite) reach the roof.

9

Potato Obstacle Race

3

Rat's Rating

Like all plants, potatoes turn energy from the sun into food energy to help them live. But what happens if you block out most of the light with obstacles? Are potatoes smart enough to get past your obstacles and reach the light?

You will need: ☆

shoebox with lid, a sprouting potato – one with little white shoots growing out of it, scissors, potting soil, "obstacles" such as small boxes, thread spools, candy tubes, baby food jars, sunny days

What to do for this biology experiment

1 Cut a small coin size gap in the short side of the box.

2 Put a handful of the potting soil in the corner of the shoebox. It must be at the opposite end from the hole you made.

3 Lay the potato on the soil.

4 Put the "obsta-cles" in the box. The smaller the box, the less obstacles you will need.

5 Put the lid on. Place the box anywhere that gets lots of sun. Don't touch the box for 4 weeks.

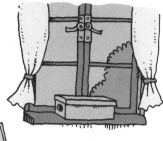

6 When the 4 weeks are up, open the box. What do you see?

What Happens

The shoot has made its way over, or around the obstacles you left in the way and has reached the hole.

Why

- Plants have cells that are sensitive to light. The cells show the plant which way to grow.
- A tiny bit of light came into the shoebox. The potato shoot twisted until it reached the light.
- Plants will always grow toward the light, even if they are buried deep in the soil.
- The shoot should be green, but it's white. This is because the *chlorophyll* that makes it green can't be made in the dark shoebox.

Fun Fact

In France, potato chips have been popular since the 1700s! It was the invention of the mechanical potato peeler in the 1920s that made potato chips go from a small specialty item to a top-selling snack food.

If I could only invent the POTATO CHIP... I could be a wealthy man! I could even be a millionaire!! But I'd need to peel faster...

Mini Quiz ?

Why is it bad to eat potatoes that have turned green?

Mini Answer ✓

Green potatoes are poisonous if you eat too many. The green is a chemical called *solanine*. This is made when the potatoes are left in sunlight. Even fluorescent lights at supermarkets can make potatoes turn green. Potato "eyes" also have lots of solanine, so don't eat them! When peeling potatoes, peel away all the green.

Cloudy Bacteria

Rat's Rating

Almost all our food has preservatives added. This is to stop food from going bad. But do preservatives really stop the growth of bacteria?

You will need:
salt, white vinegar, clear drinking glasses, chicken bouillon cube, measuring cup, measuring spoon, masking tape, marker

What to do for this zoology experiment

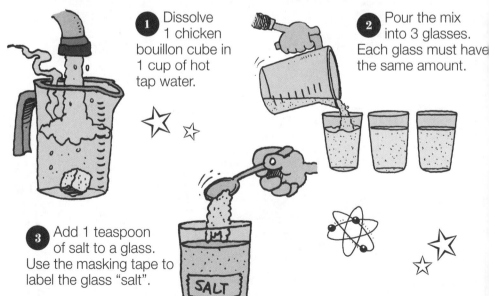

1 Dissolve 1 chicken bouillon cube in 1 cup of hot tap water.

2 Pour the mix into 3 glasses. Each glass must have the same amount.

3 Add 1 teaspoon of salt to a glass. Use the masking tape to label the glass "salt".

SALT

4 Add 1 teaspoon of vinegar to the 2nd glass. Label it "vinegar."

5 Label the 3rd glass "control", because it won't have a preservative.

6 Place the 3 glasses in a warm place. Leave them for 2 days. Which glass is cloudier?

Boy! This is a warm spot!

And we've got 2 DAYS of it!

What Happens

The glass with the vinegar is clearer than the others. The "control" is the most cloudy.

Why

- The cloudiness is made from large amounts of bacteria.
- The other two glasses have preservatives; therefore, they are clearer than the control. This is because the preservatives slow the growth of bacteria.
- Vinegar stops the bacterial growth the best.
- Food preservatives are important to help stop food from going bad. They stop the growth of molds and bacteria.

Fun Fact

Cotton dishcloths and cellulose sponges are full of bacteria. These germs can make you sick. You can kill the bacteria. Just heat the cloths and sponges for 1 minute on high in your microwave oven.

There's no way I'm trying a hot sponge out of a microwave oven without sauce!

Mini Quiz
Are preservatives in food bad for you?

Mini Answer
For most people, preservatives are safe. Other people are very sensitive or even allergic to them. This is why packaged food with preservatives must have a clear label.

Fuzz Balls

Rat's Rating

I don't like the way that mold is staring at me!

Can mold be useful in making medicine? Does bacteria have an infectious laugh? Let's find out.

You will need:

oranges, lemons, or other citrus fruits, bowl, clear polythene bags (the type bread comes in), cotton balls

Rat's Helpful Hint

If you don't have time to do this experiment, just look behind the sofa, or under your bed. You're sure to find all sorts of moldy food.

What to do for this botany experiment

1 Place the fruit in a bowl. Leave it out in the air for 1 day.

2 Open the 2 bread bags. Put 1 orange, 1 lemon, and a wet cotton ball in each bag.

3 Tie the ends of the bags.

4 Place one bag in the refrigerator.

COOL SCIENCE EXPERIMENTS

5 Place the other bag in a warm dark place.

6 Leave the bags closed for 2 weeks.

7 Check the fruit through the bags each day.

What Happens

The fruit in the refrigerator looks much the same. At worst, it may be a bit drier. The other fruit has turned into blue-green fuzz balls. This fuzzy growth on the outside of the fruit is *penicillin*.

Why

- Mold is a form of fungus that makes tiny cells called spores.
- Spores are even tinier than dust particles! They float through the air.
- Mold grows faster in moist warm places. That is why foods become moldier in the summer.
- Keeping food cool slows the growth of mold. Freezing keeps foods fresh for even longer periods.
- Fungi are all around us. They usually don't reach the fruiting body stage. This is because there aren't enough nutrients and water available.

EEEEE...! That's some mighty ugly citrus fruit!

? ? ? ?

Fun Fact

Under a microscope, penicillin mold looks like a small brush. The Latin word for paintbrush is "penicillus". This is how penicillin got its name. The word pencil also comes from this Latin word, because brushes were used for writing.

Mini Quiz ?

How did an accident lead to the discovery that penicillin could kill bacteria?

? ? ?

Mini Answer ✓

Alexander Fleming discovered penicillin by accident. In 1928, he left an open dish of bacteria in his laboratory and after two weeks found mold growing on the bacteria. He saw that there was a clear zone where the bacteria had died. Fleming discovered that the mold had made a chemical that could kill bacteria and cure infections. Penicillin is still used today as an antibiotic to fight some infections.

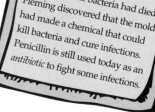

You gotta see this! There's more than PENICILLIN living in your toothbrush! Where's it been?

In my MOUTH...

6 Rock and Dissolve

Rat's Rating

Can something as soft as rain dissolve something as strong as a rock?

You will need:
small drinking glasses, glass lemon juice, glass vinegar, glass water, 3 pieces white chalk

What to do for this chemistry experiment

1 Pour ½ glass lemon juice in glass 1. Pour ½ glass vinegar in glass 2. Pour ½ glass water in glass 3.

2 Put 1 piece of chalk in each of the glasses. Make sure part of the chalk is in the liquid.

3 Place the glasses where they won't be knocked over.

4 Check on the glasses over the next few days. What is happening?

Why

- When you breathe out, you send carbon dioxide into the air.
- When carbon dioxide dissolves into raindrops, it makes rain become naturally acidic.
- Over time, this acid rain dissolves and erodes rocks.
- The chalk you used in the experiment is made of the rock limestone, or *calcium carbonate*.
- When acids react with limestone, they eat away at the rock and start to break it apart.
- Lemon juice and vinegar are acids. They're much stronger than acid rain, so erosion happens more quickly. You can see how acid rain can affect rocks over hundreds and thousands of years.

What Happens

The chalk dissolves in the vinegar and in the lemon juice.

Fun Fact

England's famous White Cliffs of Dover are made of great sheets of chalk, a form of calcium carbonate. If you lean against the cliffs, you get covered with white powder.

Mini Quiz

What does the Great Pyramid of Giza have to do with chalk?

Mini Answer ✓

The Great Pyramid is mainly made from blocks of limestone. The fine white limestone came from a quarry on the other side of the Nile. Egyptians used copper chisels to cut their way down into the limestone. They slowly separated block after block from the rock face.

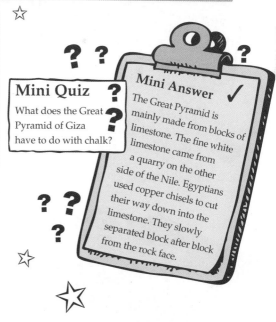

It's Not Easy Being Green

Rat's Rating

I think all you need is a little light, my friend!

"Leaf through" these green activities. You'll find that looking green doesn't always mean looking sickly.

You will need:

pieces black paper, indoor potted plant with green leaves, scissors, paperclip, tape

Rat's Helpful Hint

Make sure the plant you use is alive. If you use a fake one, not a lot will happen.

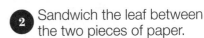

What to do for this botany experiment

1 Cut 2 pieces of black paper big enough to cover one leaf on the plant.

2 Sandwich the leaf between the two pieces of paper.

18

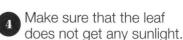

3 Clip the paper at the top and tape the sides.

4 Make sure that the leaf does not get any sunlight.

5 Wait for 7 days.

6 Uncover the leaf. Does it look different compared to the rest of the plant?

What Happens

The leaf is much paler than the other leaves in the plant. Now, watch the leaf over the next few days. See what happens to it when it gets sunlight again.

Why
- If plants don't get sunlight, they can't make chlorophyll.
- Chlorophyll is the chemical that gives leaves their green color.
- Without sunlight, the green pigment gets used up. It can't be replaced in the leaf. You end up with a leaf that loses its green color, and finally dies.
- After a week without the covering, the leaf turns green again.

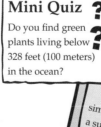

Fun Fact

Leaves are nature's food factories. Plants take water from the ground through their roots. They take a gas called *carbon dioxide* from the air. Plants use sunlight to turn water and carbon dioxide into glucose. Plants use glucose for energy and growing.

I've just spent seven days in some kind of scientific experiment... so I'm out to get some sun... Some water... and plenty of nice fresh carbon dioxide.

Mini Quiz

Do you find green plants living below 328 feet (100 meters) in the ocean?

Mini Answer

No! Green plants only grow near the surface of the ocean. The deeper the water, the less plants are found. This is because green plants need sunlight. The sunlight totally disappears below 328 feet (100 meters) and the plants cannot live. Try something similar yourself. Put one plant in a sunny spot and another plant of the same variety in a dark cupboard and leave them for 7 days. The plant in the cupboard will be lighter in color and wilted.

Fizzy, Flowing, and Funky

8

Super Starch

I may look like an uninteresting glob of cornflour ... but I can do some amazing things!

Rat's Rating

Can something be a solid and a liquid at the same time? Sounds impossible! What do you think?

You will need:
cornstarch, measuring cup, mixing spoon, bowl

What to do for this chemistry experiment

1 Place 1 cup of cornstarch in a large bowl.

2 Add about ¼ – ½ cup water and mix to a thick paste.

3 The powder is solid. The water is a liquid. Do you think the mixture will be a solid or a liquid?

4 Actually, it's both! With your hands, knead a handful of the mixture. It will become firm as long as you keep kneading.

5 Stop kneading. Quickly punch the mixture with your fist. It feels hard and may even crack.

6 Watch the mixture. Now that you have stopped kneading, it will return to its original form.

7 Push your fingers into it very slowly. They will slide in as though the mixture is a liquid. Raise your hands and see it pour through your fingers.

What Happens

As it stands, the mixture is a liquid—it's just water with powder floating in it. However, when you hit it, the water molecules are forced into the middle of each grain of powder, so the mixture is solid.

Why

- Some fluid mixtures have two forms.
- *Isotropy* is when a liquid becomes solid when moved.
- You can see this when walking on wet sand. The sand firms up below your feet when you first walk. It then becomes more liquid as your feet sink into it a moment later. If you run over the sand, it will feel hard. If you walk slowly, your feet will sink below the surface with each step.
- *Thixotropy* is the opposite of *isotropy*. *Thixotropy* is when the liquid mixture becomes more liquid as it is moved.
- You might have done this when you hit the end of a ketchup bottle to get the ketchup to come out. The force temporarily makes the ketchup "runny." and it comes out easily from the bottle.

Fun Fact

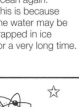

Do you know that when you drink water you're drinking dinosaur spit? The water we have today is the same water that the dinosaurs drank. How can this be? Well, it can take a water molecule thousands of years to finish a cycle from ocean to sky to land and back to the ocean again. This is because the water may be trapped in ice for a very long time.

Does your water taste a little... Prehistoric?

Sure does! A little Jurassic actually!

Mini Quiz

What does starch have to do with newspapers?

Mini Answer

Starch is used as a binder in the making of paper. It's the use of a starch coating that controls how much ink comes through when printing. Cheaper papers don't use as much starch. This is why your fingers get black when you hold newspaper.

Looks Fishy to Me

9

Rat's Rating

FISHOMETER

You have heard of fish fingers, right? Well, did you know that fish have rings too? They don't wear them on their fingers because fish don't have fingers. But they do have them on their scales. The rings are special because they tell us something about the fish.

You will need:
scales from different types of fresh fish (using just one type is fine), small piece of dark paper, microscope, or magnifying glass

Rat's Helpful Hint
Remember that no mermaid likes to give away her age. So, no pinching scales from her tail... especially when she's sitting on a rock singing.

What to do for this zoology experiment

1 Collect fish scales from your local fish market. Or, take scales from a fish in your refrigerator. Leave your pet goldfish alone!

2 Place a dried scale on the dark paper.

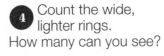

3 Use a microscope to look at the ring pattern on the scale.

4 Count the wide, lighter rings. How many can you see?

5 Count the slim, darker rings. How many can you see?

What Happens

The number of rings on the scale is equal to the age of the fish. Are there some years the fish grew fast? Are there some years it grew slow? What environmental factors might explain this?

GROWTH RINGS! I've lost count!

6 What do you think the rings show us about the fish? Why are there are two types of rings?

Why

- As a fish grows larger, the scales grow larger too.
- Scales grow by adding rings around the outside edge of the scale. These rings look like the growth rings in the trunk of a tree.
- A scale may add anywhere from two to twenty rings a year.
- More rings mean more growth.
- Small reef fish usually live for only a few weeks or months. Other fish, such as the sturgeon, can live to 50 years or more.

Fun Fact

Some Japanese restaurants serve raw puffer fish. Part of the fish is poisonous, and the chef should take this away. However, each year over 20 people die after eating the wrong parts.

AHHR-SO Pufferfish full of hot air!

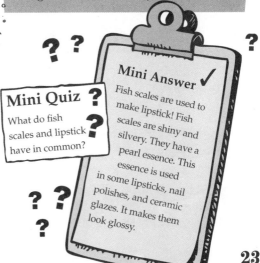

Mini Quiz ?

What do fish scales and lipstick have in common?

Mini Answer ✓

Fish scales are used to make lipstick! Fish scales are shiny and silvery. They have a pearl essence. This essence is used in some lipsticks, nail polishes, and ceramic glazes. It makes them look glossy.

Invisible Ink

Rat's Rating

"PAINTING IN INVISIBLE INK" by I.C. LITTLE

You've heard of secret messages written in code, haven't you? But have you heard of secret messages being written with invisible ink?

You will need: ☆
lemon, saucer, water, teaspoon, toothpick, white paper, lamp

Rat's Helpful Hint
Why not send your invisible ink letter to a friend to read?

What to do for this chemistry experiment

1 Squeeze the lemon juice into the saucer.

2 Add a few drops of water and mix well with the spoon.

MIX MIX

3 Dip the toothpick into the lemon juice mix. Not too much or you'll make invisible blobs!

4 Use the toothpick to write a message on ordinary white paper. Thick paper works best.

5 When it dries, the writing will be invisible.

☆

6 Heat the paper by holding it with the written side down near a light bulb. If an adult is helping, you can use heat from a stove or candle. What do you see?

What Happens

While it heats up, the invisible ink writing slowly becomes brown and visible. The words appear on the page.

This message is no longer a SECRET!

Why

- The juice of lemons has compounds of *carbon*.
- These compounds have almost no color when you dissolve them in water.
- When you heat them, the carbon compounds break down and turn black.

Fun Fact

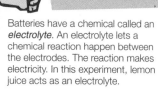

Batteries have a chemical called an *electrolyte*. An electrolyte lets a chemical reaction happen between the electrodes. The reaction makes electricity. In this experiment, lemon juice acts as an electrolyte.

My old lemons were flat in my flashlight... So I'm installing fresh ones.

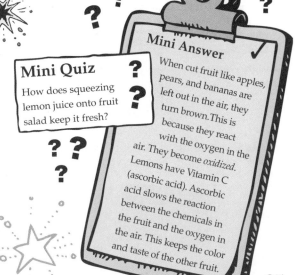

Mini Quiz

How does squeezing lemon juice onto fruit salad keep it fresh?

Mini Answer

When cut fruit like apples, pears, and bananas are left out in the air, they turn brown. This is because they react with the oxygen in the air. They become *oxidized*. Lemons have Vitamin C (ascorbic acid). Ascorbic acid slows the reaction between the chemicals in the fruit and the oxygen in the air. This keeps the color and taste of the other fruit.

Fizzy Rocket

11

Rat's Rating

Let us know if you make it to MARS!

What can fizzy tablets show us about the way rocket propellants release energy?

You will need:
antacid tablets of the same brand and type, jars, zip-up plastic bag, watch or clock with second hand, rolling pin, water

What to do for this chemistry experiment

1 Half fill 2 jars with water that is the same temperature.

2 Put 1 antacid tablet into a zip-up bag. Seal the bag.

3 Place the bag on a bench. Crush the tablet by pressing on it with the rolling pin.

26

COOL SCIENCE EXPERIMENTS

4 Open the bag with the crushed tablet. Hold it over one of the jars.

5 Get your watch ready.

6 Pour the crushed tablet into a glass with water.

7 Time how long it takes the tablet powder to dissolve.

8 Pick up a whole tablet and drop it into the 2nd glass of water.

9 Time how long it takes the powder to dissolve completely.

What Happens

The crushed antacid tablet dissolves faster.

Why

- By crushing the tablet into a powder, you've made its surface area bigger.
- The crushed tablet will now break up quickly in the water.
- The water immediately reacts with the powder.
- Rockets work in much the same way.
- The thrust of a rocket is higher when the burning surface of its fuel is higher.

Fun Fact

You can do a similar, but much tastier test with small pieces of hard candy. Take two pieces of candy and crush one. Give the whole candy piece to a friend. You keep the crushed piece. Both of you then put the candy in your mouth, but don't chew it. Let the candy dissolve in your mouth. Whose candy will dissolve first?

MM-MM....MM...M! (READY) (SET) (SUCK!)

Mini Quiz

How does the space shuttle get off the ground?

Mini Answer

Each U.S. Space Shuttle has two solid rocket boosters. These add additional thrust and acceleration to the main engines to help carry the shuttle into space. After two minutes, at an altitude of about 24 miles (38 km), the boosters separate and fall into the ocean where they are recovered and reused.

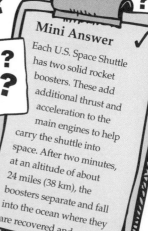

Who Won? It's a Straw

Rat's Rating

What's that? You need my STRAW for an experiment? Maybe come back later. I'm enjoying my Lemonade!

Do you think you can use a straw to pull liquid up into your mouth? No, you can't! Find out why.

You will need:
drinking straw, drinking glasses, water

What to do in this forces experiment

1 Half fill one glass with water.

2 Put the straw in the glass.

3 Suck a small amount of water into the straw.

4 Hold your finger across the top of the straw. Take the straw out of the water.

5 Place the straw over the second empty glass.

6 Take your finger away from the top of the straw. Watch the water.

What Happens
Water comes out.

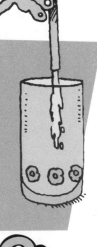

Why
- When you suck through a straw, you don't pull the liquid up. What you're doing is taking away some of the air inside the straw.
- This makes the pressure inside the straw lower than the pressure outside.
- The greater pressure of the outside air then pushes the water in the glass up through the straw and into your mouth.
- When your finger covers the top of the straw, the water stays in the straw.
- It lessens the pressure of the air from above the straw.
- The greater air pressure under the straw holds the water inside it.

Fun Fact

In 1888, Marvin Stone patented the spiral winding process to make the first paper drinking straws. Before this, drinkers used natural rye grass straws. Stone made his original straw by winding strips of paper around a pencil and gluing it together. He then used paraffin coated manila paper, so the straws wouldn't become soggy while someone was drinking. In 1906, Stone's company invented a machine to wind the straws.

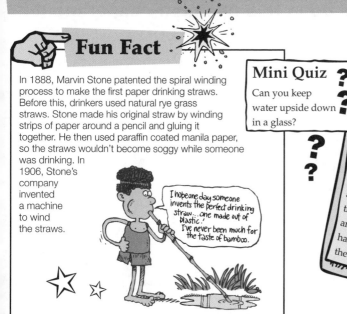

> I hope one day someone invents the perfect drinking straw... one made out of plastic. I've never been much for the taste of bamboo.

Mini Quiz ?
Can you keep water upside down in a glass?

Mini Answer ✓
Yes, you can! Fill a drinking glass completely with water. Cover the top of the glass with a piece of heavy paper. Hold it down so the card touches the rim all the way around. Turn the glass upside down and carefully remove your hand. The water stays in the glass!

13 **Let's Get Fizzy**

Rat's Rating

You've all seen fire extinguishers. They work by taking away one part needed for a fire—oxygen. Try making your own extinguisher.

You will need:
candle, tall glass jar/drinking glass, short birthday cake candle, baking powder (not soda), matches, spoon, vinegar

What to do in this chemistry experiment

You will need an adult's supervision for this experiment.

1 Get an adult to light the candle.

2 Drip some wax in the bottom of your glass jar. Blow out the candle.

3 Stick the birthday cake candle in the wax so it stands upright. Keep the tip of the candle away from the rim of the jar. Your jar must be taller than the candle.

4 Put heaping spoonfuls of baking powder into the jar. Keep the powder away from the flame as much as possible.

5 Gently pour in some vinegar. There should be enough to make the powder fizzle and pop. What happens to the candle?

☆

What Happens

After some time, the candle goes out.

Why

- Mixing the powder and the vinegar makes carbon dioxide gas.
- Unlike oxygen gas, the flame does not easily burn carbon dioxide.
- It is also heavier than the other gases that make up our atmosphere. The carbon dioxide sinks to the bottom of your jar.
- If enough gas is made, it will reach the level of the flame.
- When the candle can't keep burning its material with oxygen, it goes out.

Fun Fact

Mosquitoes don't just use their sight to find hosts to bite. They sense infra-red radiation coming from warm bodies and by chemical signals.

My INFARED RADIATION HEAT SENSORS have failed me! I'll use my eyes from now on!

Mini Quiz ?

How do fire fighters put out fire using carbon dioxide?

Mini Answer ✓

Many fire extinguishers use compressed carbon dioxide to put out fires. By filling the space around the fire with the gas, the fire is suffocated. Unfortunately, since we need oxygen gas to live, breathing pure carbon dioxide also suffocates us.

14 Eat Like a Dinosaur

Rat's Rating

Would you like a bucketful of rocks with your tree branches or whatever it is you eat?

Why would plant-eating dinosaurs swallow stones? Try this experiment to find out.

You will need: ☆

2 rounded stones or pebbles, leaves, plastic bowl, scissors, teaspoon, water

Rat's Helpful Hint

Don't ever swallow stones or you'll end up as dead as the dinosaurs.

What to do in this biology experiment

1 Put 6 small leaves in the plastic bowl.

2 Use the scissors to cut up the leaves.

3 Add ¼ teaspoon of water.

4 Hold the stones and grind the leaves between them.

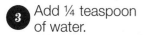

> I feel like a BRACHIOSAURUS eating lunch!

What Happens
The water turns green.

> BURP

Why
- This is what happened in the dinosaur's stomach.
- A dinosaur swallowed stones called *gastroliths* to help it eat leaves.
- As the stones released the edible parts of the leaf, bacteria in the dinosaur's stomach rotted the food. This helped the dinosaur to digest its dinner.

Fun Fact

You can make your own fossil with modeling clay and a feather or a leaf. Roll the clay flat with a rolling pin. Press the feather or a leaf as hard as you can into the clay. Remove the feather. You will see the feather is preserved in the clay.

> Now that will make A GREAT FOSSIL!

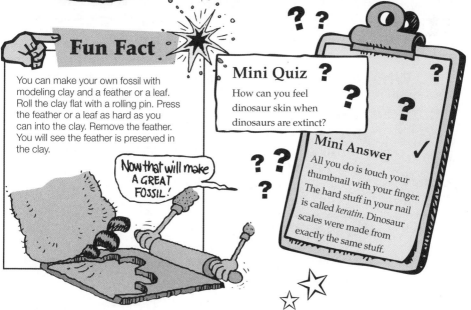

Mini Quiz
How can you feel dinosaur skin when dinosaurs are extinct?

Mini Answer ✓
All you do is touch your thumbnail with your finger. The hard stuff in your nail is called *keratin*. Dinosaur scales were made from exactly the same stuff.

(15) Red Cabbage Rules

Rat's Rating

So you reckon you're a KING? You look like a CABBAGE to me!

I'm the king of the cabbage patch.

An *indicator* is a chemical that changes color when an acid or alkali is added to it. Try making your own indicators and find out how to measure different substances.

You will need: ☆
small red cabbage, grater, bowls, water, saucepan, jug, strainer, paper towels/coffee filters, sheet of white paper, colored pencils, solution liquids to test—lemon and orange juice, vinegar, milk, tap water, soapy water, yogurt, glasses/paper cups

Rat's Helpful Hint
To stop your indicator strips from growing moldy, freeze them in bags. Remember to label the bag. If not, you may find yourself sucking on cabbage-flavored Popsicles!

What to do in this chemistry experiment

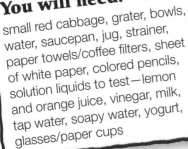

1 Grate ½ a small red cabbage. Let the gratings sit in a bowl of water for several hours. Drain the red cabbage water into another bowl. OR put the grated cabbage into a saucepan with just enough water to cover it. Ask an adult to put the pan on the stove. Boil for 20–30 minutes, until the liquid turns a dark purple color.

☆ ☆ COOL SCIENCE EXPERIMENTS

2 Let the cabbage juice cool and then strain it into a jug.

3 Cut 2 inch (5 cm) strips of paper towels.

4 Soak the strips of paper in the red cabbage juice until they turn bluish purple.

5 Lay the wet strips flat on a bench and leave them to dry. These are your indicator strips.

6 Put the liquids into separate paper cups.

7 Dip your paper indicator strips into the liquids.

LEMON | ORANGE | VINEGAR | MILK | TAP WATER | SOAPY WATER

8 Using pencils and the white paper, copy down the color that the paper strip turns.

9 Draw a picture, or write the name of the liquid that made the paper turn that color.

10 Use your notes to make a chart to show the different colors that different liquids turn the paper strips.

MY INDICATOR CHART

LEMON | ORANGE | VINEGAR | MILK

TAP WATER | SOAPY WATER | pH TESTER

What Happens

Your cabbage juice is a simple pH tester. It reacts differently to different substances. Once you know what color the juice turns in acids and alkalis, you can use it to test some other liquids.

Why

- Red cabbage has pigments that react differently to acids and alkalis.
- When you dip your strips into your substance and wait a few minutes, the color will fully develop.
- Your indicator strips will turn red-yellow in acid, green in neutral and purple blue in alkali.

Mini Quiz

What do all the colors mean on the pH scale?

Mini Answer

Scientists invented the pH scale to tell you just how acidic a substance is. The scale goes from 1, which is very acidic, through to 14, which is very alkaline. A pH of 7 is right in the middle of the scale and means a substance is neutral.

Blow Your Top

16

OOHH! That must have been a terrible headache!

Have you seen a real volcanoes erupt? Well, make your own. It's much safer.

You will need: ☆

flour, salt, cooking oil, water, large bowl, clean plastic soda bottle, baking pan, food coloring—red looks good—liquid detergent, baking soda, vinegar, water

Rat's Helpful Hint

This is a messy experiment. Make sure you know who's going to be cleaning up. Don't let your dog be the one to lick up the mess.

What to do in this chemistry experiment

1 Mix 6 cups of flour, 2 cups of salt, 4 tablespoons of cooking oil, and 2 cups of water in a large bowl.

2 Using your hands, mix the ingredients until smooth and firm. Add more water to the mixture if needed.

3 Stand the soda bottle in the baking pan.

4 Mold the salt dough around the bottle. Make sure you don't cover up the bottle mouth or drop any dough in the bottle. You can build your volcano with as much detail as you like, or leave it plain.

6 Add drops of food coloring until you get a color you like.

7 Squeeze 6 drops of the liquid detergent into the bottle.

8 Add 2 tablespoons of baking soda.

5 Fill the bottle almost to the top with warm water.

9 Slowly pour vinegar into the bottle and jump back quickly. What do you think will happen?

Why

- Mixing baking soda and vinegar makes a chemical reaction.
- A chemical reaction is where one substance is chemically changed to another.
- All chemical reactions are about the making or destroying of bonds between atoms in which carbon dioxide gas is made—the same gas that bubbles in a real volcano.
- The gas bubbles build up in the bottle. They force the liquid "lava" mixture up and over the mouth of your volcano.

What Happens

The "lava" flows out of your volcano.

VESUVIUS erupting NOW!

Fun Fact

Over the long term, volcanic eruptions can help us. Volcanic materials break down and weather so that they form fertile soils.

Yep! This should be a great place for a farm... in about a MILLION YEARS

Mini Quiz

Where does the word "volcano" come from?

Mini Answer ✓

The word "volcano" comes from the island of Vulcano, near Sicily in Italy. A century ago, the local people believed that Vulcano was the chimney of the forge of Vulcan. Vulcan was the blacksmith of the Roman gods.

17 One Dirty Hanky

Rat's Rating

Could I interest you in one of my CRINKLE CUT CRISPS?

I DON'T MIND IF I DO!

Feeling energetic? It might be thanks to all those potatoes you've been eating! Let's see how.

You will need:
large potatoes, vegetable peeler, chopping board, grater, large clean handkerchief, small mixing bowl, water

What to do in this chemistry experiment

1 Ask an adult to help you peel and grate 3 large potatoes over a chopping board.

3 Put the grated potato into the handkerchief. Tie up the handkerchief.

4 Dip the handkerchief into the water. Squeeze it very hard into the bowl.

2 Half fill the bowl with water.

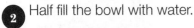

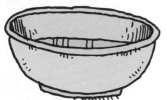

5 Keep dipping the handkerchief into the water and squeezing it out after each dipping. What is happening to the water? Is it very cloudy?

6 Leave the water in the bowl for 1 hour.

7 Can you see the white powder that has settled on the bottom of the bowl?

8 Carefully pour off as much of the clear water above the powder as you can. Leave the powder a couple of hours to dry out. What have you made?

Why
- Plants and animals make starch as a way of storing sugars.
- Potatoes, rice, barley, and wheat have large amounts of starch.
- When you eat foods high in starch, chemicals in your digestive juices change the starch to sugars that can be used by your body for quick energy.
- Starch is also put on cloth to give it weight and make it smooth. The starch you have made can be used this way when the cloth is ironed.

What Happens
The powder you have made is *starch*.

Fun Fact

A soda cracker is made of flour (which is a starch), water, and baking powder. It has no sugar. If you chew a cracker and hold it in your mouth for 5 minutes, the taste of the cracker changes. There is a special chemical in your saliva that breaks the links in the starch chains so those sugar molecules are released.

Mini Quiz
What does starch have to do with adhesive paste?

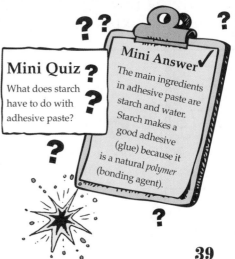

Mini Answer ✓
The main ingredients in adhesive paste are starch and water. Starch makes a good adhesive (glue) because it is a natural *polymer* (bonding agent).

39

On Your Mark—Go!

18

Rat's Rating

If I were a GAMBLING RAT and not a LAB RAT. My money would be on this speedy looking black pen over here

You've heard of horse racing and car racing, but did you know that marker pens could race each other?

You will need:

4 different brands of black markers, white coffee filter paper/ paper towels, clear drinking glass, pencil, clothespins

What to do in this biology experiment

1 Cut a rectangle out of the coffee filter. The width of the paper must fit easily in the glass. But the top of the filter paper must stick out!

3 Using each black marker place a small dot along the line. Don't put the dots too close together.

4 Put the filter paper in the glass.

2 Using a pencil, draw a line about 1 inch (2.5 cm) up from the bottom of the filter paper.

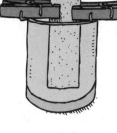

5 Clip the clothespins to the paper. Rest the clothespins across the top of the glass to stop the paper from slipping down.

6 Adjust the clothespins so the filter paper just touches the bottom of the glass.

7 Lift the filter paper out without unclipping the clothespins. Put it to one side.

8 Put a ¼ inch (.05 cm) of water in the glass.

9 Put the glass in a place where it won't be bumped.

10 Slowly and carefully, lower the filter paper back into the glass. The clothespins will stop it from slipping down.

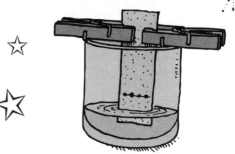

11 Don't touch the experiment, or it will go crazy!

12 Wait 5 minutes and see what has happened. Check again in another 5 minutes. Do you think the different black dots will do different things?

13 Once any changes have stopped, take the filter paper out of the glass or it will ruin the experiment.

What Happens

You will start to see different colors. Some of the markers might reach the top faster than others, or some might be more colorful. It all depends on what pens you use.

Why

- Most black markers are made from colored pigments or dyes, and water.
- The water in the ink carries the pigments up the filter paper.
- As the water dries, the pigments stay on the paper.
- The pigments dissolve when the filter is dipped in water.
- Some pigments move up the paper faster than others. They travel at different speeds. This depends on how large the pigment molecule is and how much the pigment is attracted to the paper.

Mini Quiz ?

How does ink get its color?

Mini Answer ✓

Ink gets its color by absorbing some of the colors in white light and reflecting others.

19

Are You Absorbing This?

Rat's Rating

Your intestines play a major role in absorbing the food you eat. Let's see how they work.

You will need:
masking tape, narrow glass jar, water, paper towels, marker

What to do in this biology experiment

1 Stick a piece of masking tape down the side of the jar.

2 Fill the jar with water. Mark the level on the tape with your marker.

3 Fold one sheet of paper towel in half four times to make a small square.

4 Dip the paper square into the jar of water. Make sure all the paper is under water.

5 Remove the wet paper. Mark the new water level on the tape.

6 Refill the jar with water to the same level as before.

7 Lay three sheets of paper towels on top of each other.

8 Fold them in half four times to make a small square.

9 Dip the paper square into the water.

10 Remove the wet paper. Mark the water level.

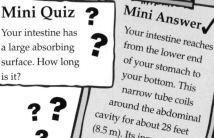
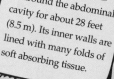

What Happens

The three sheets of folded paper towels removed much more water than the one sheet.

Why

- Folding the three sheets of paper made them smaller. But it did not change the way they soaked up water.
- The folded sheets act like the tissue inside the intestines of animals. Both are able to absorb large quantities of liquid. This is because of the makeup of their cells and their available surface area.

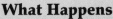

Fun Fact

Some materials absorb water better than others. Use a rubber band to tie different types of material (cotton, wool, cheesecloth, leather, fleece) to the top of clean empty jars. Carefully drip one teaspoon of water onto each jar. Do this a few times. Take away the material. See which jars have the most water. These materials will be less absorbent. The jars with very little water inside have absorbent material.

Mini Quiz
Your intestine has a large absorbing surface. How long is it?

Mini Answer ✓
Your intestine reaches from the lower end of your stomach to your bottom. This narrow tube coils around the abdominal cavity for about 28 feet (8.5 m). Its inner walls are lined with many folds of soft absorbing tissue.

Who's the anti-social jar down the end with the lid on?

Wax Factor

**Can you make a
new candle from
bits and pieces
of old ones?**

WOOPS! Forgot to pay the LAB'S POWER BILL!

You will need:
pieces of old, used white candles, old, used wax crayons, pan, string, spoon, skewer, paper cup

What to do for this chemistry experiment

1 Put the candles and the wax crayons in a pan.

2 Ask an adult to melt them slowly over a low heat. Stir gently to swirl the mix together.

3 While the wax is melting, make a small hole in the bottom of a paper cup with a skewer.

4 Thread the string through.

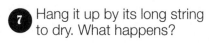
5 Tie a knot underneath. The string should be long enough so you can hang your candle to dry.

6 Ask an adult to pour the wax into the paper cup.

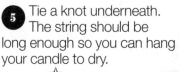

7 Hang it up by its long string to dry. What happens?

What Happens

The wax will turn hard. To use your new candle, snip the string at the top and the bottom. Leave just enough at the top to use for the wick. It is very IMPORTANT to remove the paper cup before you light your new candle.

Why

- Wax can change from a solid to a liquid when it is heated.
- It will become a solid again when it cools.

SNIP

Fun Fact

On Earth, gravity-driven buoyant convection makes a candle flame a teardrop-shape. This means that the air in the flame expands and becomes lighter. The lighter air rises up. This is the convection current. In microgravity, there are no convective flows. The candle flame is round because the vaporized wax spreads out from the wick and the oxygen goes into the flame from surrounding air.

Do you mind if I blow out the candles now before they burn out... And we discuss the finer points of GRAVITY-DRIVEN BUOYANT CONVECTION a little later!

Mini Quiz

Where do candles come from?

Mini Answer ✓

Candles came from the Romans. Ancient Egyptians used tallow-soaked torches, but the Romans had candles with a wick. These were used to help people travel through dark nights, light homes and places of worship.

Streaky Paper

Rat's Rating

GGRRRRR

Want to wrap a small gift but don't have any wrapping paper? Try making your own by using ordinary sheets of white paper. Here's how.

You will need:

color chalk—go for colors that will look good together, white paper—amount depends on how much swirly paper you want to make, paper or plastic cups, rolling pin, vinegar, zip-lock plastic bags, plastic spoon, large plastic bowl, newspaper, water, cooking oil

What to do in this chemistry experiment

1 Place sheets of newspaper on a table.

2 Fill the bowl with water.

3 Add 2 tablespoons of vinegar.

4 Place the bowl in the center of the newspaper.

5 Place small pieces of different colored chalk into separate zip-lock bags. Zip up the bag.

6 Use the rolling pin to crush the chalk into a fine powder.

7 Tip each powered chalk color into its own cup.

8 Pour 1 tablespoon of oil into each cup. Stir well with the plastic spoon.

9 Pour the contents of each cup into the bowl of water. The chalky colored oil should form large colored pools on top of the water.

10 Carefully lay each piece of of white paper on the surface the water.

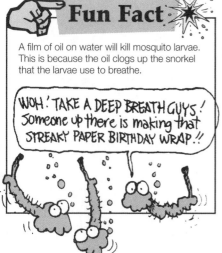

11 Lift out and place on the sheets of newspaper to dry. This will take about 24 hours.

12 When the papers are fully dried, carefully wipe off any surface chalk grains with a paper towel. What do you have left?

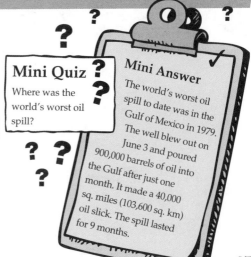

What Happens

The colored oil sticks to the paper and makes swirls and streaky patterns.

Why

- Negative and positive charged molecules are attracted to each other.
- The molecules of chalk (calcium carbonate) and vinegar (acetic acid) and water and the surface of the paper all chemically mix to make a chemical bond.
- This causes the streaky colors to stick to the paper.

Fun Fact

A film of oil on water will kill mosquito larvae. This is because the oil clogs up the snorkel that the larvae use to breathe.

WOH! TAKE A DEEP BREATH GUYS! Someone up there is making that STREAKY PAPER BIRTHDAY WRAP.!!

Mini Quiz

Where was the world's worst oil spill?

Mini Answer

The world's worst oil spill to date was in the Gulf of Mexico in 1979. The well blew out on June 3 and poured 900,000 barrels of oil into the Gulf after just one month. It made a 40,000 sq. miles (103,600 sq. km) oil slick. The spill lasted for 9 months.

Gelatin Mobile

Rat's Rating

You're going to have to stop being so nervous and stop wobbling like jelly... you'll ruin the photo!

Gelatin is used to make pill capsules, heart valves, photographic film, and of course fruit-flavored desserts. But can you make a mobile with it?

You will need:
plain gelatin, water, food color, plastic lid with rim, saucepan, egg slice, paper towels, cookie cutters, drinking straw, scissors, cooling rack

Rat's Helpful Hint
Why not color your mobile to match a festivity such as orange for Halloween, red for Valentine's Day or green for St. Patrick's Day?

What to do in this chemistry experiment

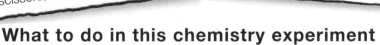

1 Put 5 tablespoons (75 ml) of water and 3–5 drops of food coloring in the saucepan.

2 Ask an adult to put the saucepan over a low heat.

3 Tip in the 3 envelopes of unflavored gelatin and stir until it dissolves.

4 Cook and stir for 30 seconds or until the mixture is thick.

COOL SCIENCE EXPERIMENTS

5 Pour the mixture into a plastic lid with a rim.

7 Let the gelatin cool for 45 minutes.

6 Push the air bubbles out with a spoon.

8 Use an egg slice to carefully lift the gelatin from the lid. What have you made?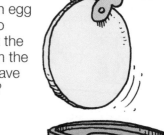

What Happens

You have made an elastic gel. Use the cookie cutters to make different shapes. Scissors are great for making spirals. Make holes in the gel with a plastic drinking straw so you can hang your shapes. Dry your shapes on a cooling rack, or hang them on string to dry. The gelatin will be hard like plastic in 2–3 days.

Why

- Gelatin is actually a protein called *collagen.*
- Collagen molecules line up to make fibers. These fibers don't dissolve in water.
- The fibers form a network that hold cells in place.
- When collagen is heated, it breaks down to make a simpler protein called gelatin.
- Gelatin does dissolve in water. When a gelatin solution cools, it makes a semi-solid mass or gel.
- A network of gelatin molecules trap the water in gelatin. It does this in much the same way as collagen molecules trap water.

Fun Fact

When connected to an EEG (electroencephalogram) machine, gelatin shows movement almost the same as the brain waves of a healthy adult.

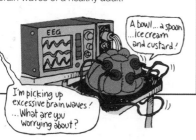

A bowl... a spoon ...ice cream and custard!

I'm picking up excessive brain waves! ...What are you worrying about?

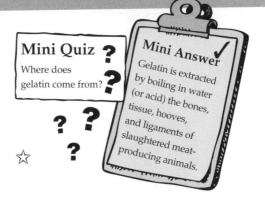

Mini Quiz Where does gelatin come from?

Mini Answer Gelatin is extracted by boiling in water (or acid) the bones, tissue, hooves, and ligaments of slaughtered meat-producing animals.

23 Save Our Silver

Rat's Rating

NOW.... NOW! We don't use silver relics for Scientific Experiments!

Silver is a bright and shiny metal. But it becomes stained when it reacts with sulfur in the air. Can you save the silver from being stained forever?

You will need:

dirty piece of silver, big bowl, aluminum foil, water, electric jug/microwave oven, kitchen mitts, baking soda

What to do

1 Line the bottom of the bowl with the aluminum foil.

2 Place your piece of silver on top of the foil. Make sure the silver touches the foil.

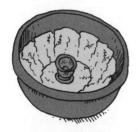

3 Ask an adult to heat the water to boiling.

4 Remove the water from the heat and place it in a sink.

5 Add about ½ cup of baking soda for each ½ gallon (1.2 litre) of water. The mixture will froth a bit and may spill over. This is why you put it in the sink!

6 Pour the hot baking soda and water mixture into the bowl. Make sure the silver is completely covered. Can you see any change in the silver?

What Happens

e stain begins to appear. If the silver is ly lightly stained, all of e stain will disappear thin several minutes. he silver is badly ained, you may need to eat the baking soda d water mixture, and e the silver several atments to remove all the stain.

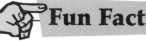

BEFORE   AFTER

Why

- When silver stains, it mixes with sulfur and makes *silver sulfide.*
- Silver sulfide is black. When a thin coating of silver sulfide forms on the surface of silver, it makes the silver all dark.
- You used a chemical reaction to change the silver sulfide back into silver.
- The silver sulfide reacted with the aluminum foil. In the reaction, sulfur atoms moved from silver to aluminum. This frees the silver metal and makes aluminum sulfide.
- The reaction between silver sulfide and aluminum takes place when both are in the baking soda. The reaction is faster when the solution is warm. The baking powder mix carries the sulfur from the silver to the aluminum. The aluminum sulfide sticks to the aluminum foil.
- The silver and aluminum must be in contact with each other. This is because a small electric current flows between them during the reaction. This is called an *electrochemical reaction.* Reactions like this are used in batteries to make electricity.

Fun Fact

Did you know that bacteria in our mouths feed on left-over food particles and make smelly sulfur compounds? These sulfur compounds give breath its bad smell.

I just had the most yummy bit of cherry pie !

Well, remember that T-Bone steak last Tuesday? It's doing quite nicely over here.

Mini Quiz

Why is silver so shiny? **?**

Mini Answer

Silver is shiny because it is a very reflective metal. This means it can be polished to "give back" as much light as hits it.

Twister

Rat's Rating

WHOA! What have I created? A TWISTER? Oh... It's only a Mobius strip!

Can there ever be a place where inside and outside is one and the same?

You will need:
sheet of paper, scissors, pen, masking tape

What to do in this topology experiment

1 Cut the paper into a long rectangle about 1 inch (2 cm) wide.

3 Give it a half twist (180 degrees). Use the masking tape to stick the two ends together.

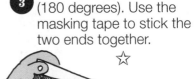

2 Hold the strip out straight.

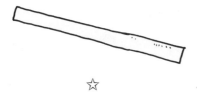

4 Hold the edge of the strip against the tip of a pen.

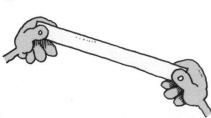

5 Draw a line down the center of the strip. Don't take the pen off the paper.

6 Turn the paper and keep on drawing the line. You will move the paper as you go along. Do not stop until your line meets up with your starting point.

7 Take off the masking tape. Look at the paper. What have you done?

What Happens

You have drawn on both sides of the paper without lifting your pen! Now, tape it back how it was before (with a half twist). With the scissors, cut the strip along the center line that you drew. Can you guess what you will make? You have made a chain that is twice as long as your original loop!

Why

- Your shape is known as a *Mobius* strip.
- When you twisted your strip, the inside and outside became one continuous surface.
- When you cut the strip, it became one longer chain. But it still had only one continuous surface.
- Now, try the experiment again. This time give the paper a full twist. You'll be surprised at what you see.

Fun Fact

During the early 1800s, the German mathematician August Mobius helped develop a study in geometry that is known as *topology*. Topology explores the properties of a geometrical figure that do not change when the figure is bent, or stretched.

I don't know what I'm making! I was going to call it a MOBIUS STRIP... But I think I'll just call it .... a mess!

Mini Quiz?

Can Mobius strips be used for anything?

Mini Answer ✓

Mobius strips have been used as fan belts in cars and conveyor belts in factories. You'll find them being used as continuous loop recording tapes. This doubles the playing time of the tapes.

25 Fantastic Plastic

Rat's Rating

A bottle of milk and a plastic bag ...all in one!

Plastic can be natural when it's made from something like oil or synthetic when made from material like nylon. But can plastic come from something as natural as milk?

You will need:
full cream milk, measuring cup, small saucepan, small jar, vinegar, tea strainer

What to do in this chemistry experiment

1 Pour ½ cup milk (125 mls) into a small saucepan.

2 Ask an adult to heat the milk until it simmers.

3 When the milk curdles and goes lumpy, stir in 3 teaspoons of vinegar.

4 Keep adding more vinegar until the mixture starts to gel.

5 Ask an adult to take the saucepan off the heat.

6 Pour off the liquid through a tea strainer.

7 Tip the lumps of curd into a jar.

8 Wait about 1 hour for the lumps to cool.

9 Slowly pour off any more water. What do you have left?

Why

- The plastic forms because of a chemical reaction.
- This reaction is between the casein in the milk and the *acetic* acid in the vinegar.
- When the milk and acid interacts, the milk separates.
- It separates into a liquid and a solid made of fat, minerals, and protein casein. This is made up of very long molecules that bend like rubber until they become hard. The same thing happens when milk curdles.

What Happens

You've made plastic! Why not dress up like Miss Muffet? You can sit outside with your plastic curds and see if a plastic spider comes along to eat them!

I might be a plastic spider... But that doesn't mean I have to like eating PLASTIC!

Fun Fact

Plastic bags and other plastic garbage thrown into the ocean kill as many as 1,000,000 sea creatures every year!

Mini Quiz

It takes five years for a milk carton to break down and return to the Earth. How long does a plastic bag take?

Mini Answer ✓

It takes 400 years for a plastic sandwich bag to break down and return to the Earth.

All Fall Down

26 The Suspenseful Egg

Go on...
Jump in...
Do a few laps!
The water's nice!

Can you imagine something that doesn't float or sink when put in a liquid?

You will need:
large glass jar, egg, water, teaspoon, salt

What to do in this forces experiment

1 Half fill a glass jar with freshwater. Put a raw egg into the jar. It sinks, doesn't it?

2 Take out the egg.

3 Add 2 teaspoons of salt to the water. Mix well.

4 Take the same egg and put it in the jar. Watch the egg. What happens?

What Happens

If there is enough salt in the water, the egg will float.

Why

• The egg floats in saltwater because of density (weight divided by the amount of space it occupies). The egg has greater density than freshwater, so it sinks.

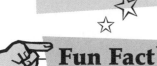 **Fun Fact**

The surface of the Earth is 75 percent covered with water. Of all that water, 97 percent of it is saltwater. We can't drink saltwater. It is hard and costs a lot of money to take away salt from the water to make it drinkable.

Mini Quiz

Why does ocean water contain salt?

Mini Answer

As water flows in rivers, it picks up small amounts of mineral salts from the rocks and soil of the riverbeds. This slightly salty water flows into the ocean. The water in the ocean only leaves by evaporating and freezing as polar ice, but the salt stays dissolved in the ocean. It does not evaporate. The water that's left grows saltier and saltier as time passes.

OH GREAT! Most people struggle through the burning desert to a cool shady oasis.... It's just my luck to arrive at a FRESH WARM GLASS OF SEA WATER!

FRESH WARM SEA WATER

Loop the Loop

Rat's Rating

So what are your thoughts on becoming the first toy dog in orbit..?

Ever wondered how satellites stay in orbit? Or why laundry in a washing machine is pushed against the sides during the spin cycle? Two forces—that of *gravity* and *centrifugal* force—are the reason. Try these experiments to see how these forces work.

You will need:

rope 24 inches (60 cm) long, bucket, soft ☆ rubber ball

Rat's Helpful Hint

Test forces at a fair or theme park. Go on one of those rides where you stand up while spinning around and the floor drops out from underneath you. It's another fun way to test forces.

What to do in your forces experiment

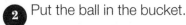

1 Tie the rope tightly to the handle of the bucket.

2 Put the ball in the bucket.

3 Go outside where there is no risk of you hitting anything.

4 Hold the bucket by the rope.

5 Whirl the bucket in the air as fast as you can.

What Happens

If you haven't hit anything, or anyone, the ball will stay in the bucket even when it turns upside down. For a satellite, it's the gravity of Earth, and not a string, that stops it flying out of orbit.

Why

- Centrifugal force – the force made by the whirling action – equals the force of gravity.
- This keeps the ball from falling out of the bucket.
- It pulls the ball against the sides of the bucket rather than down and out of it.
- Centrifugal force is directed away from the center by the rotating bucket. It is a "fleeing from the center" force.

Fun Fact

Want to feel the force of energy? Stretch a rubber band out suddenly. Then place it against your cheek. Feel the warmth? That is the stored energy trying to escape as heat!

What are you trying to do with that rubber band? Show energy escaping as heat?

NO... IT'S OUT OF CONTROL... WE'RE HEADING FOR A MELTDOWN!!

Mini Quiz

What is the difference between *centripetal* force and *centrifugal* force?

Mini Answer

Tie a ball to a long piece of string. Spin it around over your head. Centripetal force tries to pull the ball inward towards the center of the spin. Centrifugal force tries to throw the ball off in a straight line.

59

Candles Rock

28

Rat's Rating

I don't see any of you candles ROCKING! Maybe it's just not that sort of rock!

The center of gravity is that point in an object where there is as much weight on one side as the other.

You will need:
blunt knife or scissors, long candle, long nail, drinking glasses, saucers

What to do in this forces experiment

1 Scrape away some wax from the flat end of the candle so you can see the wick.

2 Push a long nail through the exact middle of the candle.

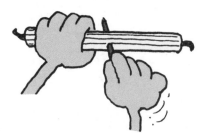

3 Rest the nail over both glasses.

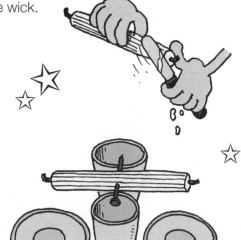

4 Put the saucers under each end of the candle.

5 Now you have a seesaw, but can you make it rock?

6 Ask an adult to light the wicks at both ends. Watch and see what happens.

What Happens
The candle rocks up and down.

Why
- A drop of hot wax falls from one end of the candle. This end rises because it is a bit lighter. Moments later, a drop falls from the other end of the candle, and so it goes on.
- The balance of the candle is always being upset. This results in the candle continuing to rock up and down.

Fun Fact

If you lay a potted plant on its side and leave it for a week, something amazing happens. The plant's stem will turn upwards! Plants have a chemical called auxin. This makes plant cells grow long. Gravity pulls the auxin down. This builds-up along the bottom of the stem. The cells grow longer where the auxin build-up makes the stem turn upward.

Mini Quiz
Do men and women have a different center of gravity?

Mini Answer
Yes, they do! Most women have their center of gravity in the hip area. Men have it in their upper body. Try it yourself. Stand with your toes touching a wall. Place one foot behind the other. Take three steps back from the wall. Have someone place a stool between you and the wall. Lean over and place the top of your head against the wall. Your legs should be at about a 45-degree angle with your body. Holding the edge of the stool, pick it up, and hold the seat against your chest. Keeping the stool against your chest, try to stand up. If you have a low center of gravity (female), the weight of the stool will not stop you standing up. If you have a high center of gravity (male), the weight of the stool makes you so top heavy that you can't stand up.

OK! Obviously a plant with more than its fair share of AUXIN!

29

Are You a Swing King?

I hope this experiment is over before midnight!

How does playing on a swing teach you something about science? Well, a swing is a *pendulum.* You're going to test whether weight will change the speed of the swing.

You will need:
a watch, outside playground swing, ruler, 2 friends

What to do in this forces experiment

1 Hold the seat of the swing and move back 3 or 4 steps.

2 Ask your friend to put the ruler on the ground in front of your feet.

3 Using the watch, your friend is to start timing when you let go of the swing. Don't push the swing, just let it go. Count the number of times the swing goes back and forth in 10 seconds.

COOL SCIENCE EXPERIMENTS

4 Your friend must call out when 10 seconds is up.

5 Ask your other friend to sit on the swing.

6 Pull the swing back until your feet are behind the ruler like the first time.

7 Have your friend start timing when you let go of the swing. Don't push the swing. Count the number of times the swing goes back and forth in the 10 seconds.

What Happens
The number of back and forth swings are the same.

Why
- Gravity pulls on the swing. It makes the swing fall when you let it go.
- The speed during the swing did change. However, the change was the same for each weight.
- The speed was faster as the swing got close to the upright position.
- It slowed as it moved upward where it stopped.
- Pendulums stop at the highest position of their swing before beginning the downward swing regardless of weight.

Fun Fact

In 1656, the Dutch scientist, Christiaan Huygens, made the first pendulum clock. This was much more accurate in measuring time than earlier clocks. Later, he invented the balance wheel and spring assembly, which is still used in watches today!

Mini Quiz
How long does it take the Earth to spin around once?

Mini Answer ✓
It takes the Earth one day (24 hours) to spin around once.

Pen Cap Submarine

30

Rat's Rating

How can a submarine sink in the ocean, then rise again and float on top?

You will need:
small clear plastic soda bottle, modeling clay, plastic pen cap, water

What to do in this forces experiment

1 Fill the clean plastic bottle with water.

3 Put the cap in the bottle so that it floats.

2 Put a piece of modeling clay on the arm of a plastic pen cap.

4 Put the lid on the bottle. It must be tight so that air doesn't leak from the bottle.

5 Squeeze the sides of the bottle. What do you think will happen?

Why

- When you squeeze the bottle, you make more pressure inside.
- This forces more water up into the pen cap.
- The added water in the pen cap makes it weigh more. This makes the cap sink.
- A submarine works in much the same way. Each submarine has tanks that can be filled with water, or air.
- When filled with air, the submarine will float on the surface of the water.
- When the submarine dives, large amounts of water are pumped into the tanks. This makes it much heavier.
- By regulating the amount of water and air in the tanks, the crew of the submarine can make it rise or sink to whatever level they want.

What Happens

The pen cap sinks when you squeeze the sides of the bottle.

Fun Fact

In the bathtub, pierce a hole in the lid and bottom of a plastic bottle. Push a plastic tube through the hole in the lid. Put your finger over the hole in the bottom. Fill the bottle to the top with water. Screw on the lid. Let the bottle sink to the bottom of the bath. Take your finger away from the hole and blow into the tube.
Your mini-sub will rise to the surface.

Mini Quiz

Are submarines a modern invention?

Mini Answer ✓

No! Greeks and Romans wrote about diving bells, and so did medieval writers. An English inventor described a workable submarine in 1578, and a Dutch inventor finally built oar-driven submarines in the early 1600s.

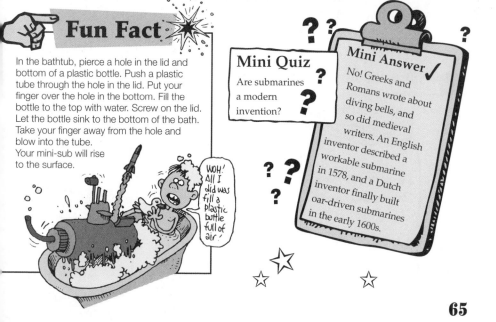

WOH! All I did was fill a plastic bottle full of air.

Pop Up Ball

31

Boiled rice...
Fried rice...
...a nice
rice pudding?
I must stop
thinking of
my stomach..
This rice must
be used
for
SCIENCE!

Why do solids of different sizes and shapes separate as they heap together?

You will need:
large glass jar with a wide mouth, uncooked rice, small rubber ball

What to do in this chemistry experiment

1 Fill ¾ of the jar with rice.

2 Put the ball in the jar. Push it down so that it is buried in the rice.

BALL

3 Place the jar on the table. Shake it back and forth. What will happen to the ball?

What Happens

The ball comes to the top of the jar!

Why

- In any mix of solids there are spaces in-between the pieces.
- When your mix is shaken, the grains rearrange themselves.
- Gravity forces the grains downward.
- The grain needs a space to move into.
- As you shake the jar, each rice grain finds a space. But there is never a space big enough for the ball.
- As the ball moves up, rice grains settle underneath. They stop the ball from moving back down. With each shake, the ball moves up, but not down.
- After a few minutes of shaking, the ball comes out from the rice and sits on top.

Fun Fact

You can use mixed nuts to see another example of separation. Shake the can of nuts. Open them. The bigger nuts like Brazil Nuts will be at the top. The smaller nuts will mainly be on the bottom.

Hey sonny...
Keep shaking that can!
It's bringing all my favorite Brazil Nuts to the top!

Mini Quiz
Why is rice thrown at a wedding?

Mini Answer ✓
The custom comes from the ancient Hindus and Chinese. In these cultures, rice is the symbol of success. Today, throwing rice is being replaced by birdseed. This is because uncooked rice hurts the birds that eat it.

Hot Stuff

Kaboom

32

Rat's Rating

How can water float on water? Make your own underwater volcano and find out.

You will need:

small glass bottle, water, food coloring, string, large glass jar (big enough for the bottle to fit inside), scissors

What to do in this heat experiment

1 Cut a long piece of string. Tie one end tightly around the neck of the bottle.

2 Tie the other end of the string around the neck of the bottle to make a loop.

COOL SCIENCE EXPERIMENTS

3 Pour cold water into the large glass jar until it is about ¾ full.

4 Fill the small glass bottle with hot water.

5 Add food coloring – red looks good!

6 Hold the bottle by the loop of the string.

7 Gently lower it into the jar of cold water.

What Happens

The hot red water rises from the bottle like smoke from an erupting volcano.

Why

- The water looks as if it is still, but it isn't!
- Its molecules are always moving.
- Molecules move more quickly when they are hot.
- Hot water always rises to the surface and floats on the cold water.
- Cooler molecules sink.

Fun Fact

The Mid-Ocean Ridge is the biggest mountain range on our planet. It's more than 30,000 miles (48,280 km) long and almost 500 miles (804 km) wide. Nearly every day, at least one underwater volcano erupts.

Mini Quiz ?

How can a volcano erupt underwater?

Mini Answer ✓

An underwater volcano can erupt underwater because it is not a fire. Fire is a chemical reaction. It needs oxygen to keep going. If you put a fire underwater, you take away the source of oxygen. The chemical reaction stops. Underwater volcanoes are very different. What you see on the surface is material that is already hot. It doesn't need any reaction at the surface to make it hot. There isn't any way for the water to "put out" the eruption. This is because the water is changed to steam, which then explodes.

QUICK! RUN!...I mean SWIM FOR YOUR LIFE! IT'S ABOUT TO BLOW!!

69

Hot Diggity Dog

(33)

Rat's Rating

YUM! THERE'S NOTHING LIKE...
............an empty pizza box!

Solar energy can change directly or indirectly into other forms of energy, such as heat and electricity. But can you cook with it? Make a solar oven and find out.

You will need:

a very hot sunny day, pizza box, black construction paper, wide aluminum foil sheet, plastic, glue, tape, scissors, ruler, marker, string, nail, skewer, choice of food to cook—hot dogs/pancakes

What to do in this heat experiment

1 Tape the foil to the inside bottom of the clean pizza box.

2 Cover the foil with the black paper. Tape it down.

3 Put the box on the sheet of plastic.

4 Draw the outline of the box on the sheet of plastic with the marker.

5 Cut the plastic about ¼ inch (0.5 cm) inside the marks.

CUT 0.5cm in from PEN LINE

6 On the top of the box, draw a line 1 inch (10 cm) from all sides.

7 Cut along the front and side lines. Do not cut along the back. This will be the hinge for the flap. Carefully fold open the flap.

8 Cut a piece of foil the same size as the flap. Glue it to the side of the flap that faces into the box. Flatten out any wrinkles.

FOIL

9 Wipe any glue off with a damp towel before it dries.

10 Tape the plastic to the inside of the box. Make it tight so it looks like glass.

TAPE PLASTIC ON HERE   FOIL

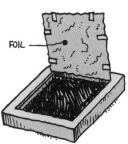

11 Tape the other edges. Make sure it is tight so no air can get in.

12 Cut a piece of string as long as the box. Tape one end to the top of the flap.

13 Push a small nail into the back of the box so you have a place to tie the string.

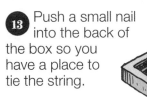

14 Poke a metal skewer through the middle of your hot dog. It will cook more quickly if cut in half.

15 Put the hot dog in your solar oven. Place the oven in a hot spot. The sun needs to shine right into the box. The best time to use your solar oven is between 12 and 2.00 p.m. This is when the sun is at its strongest.

SIZZLE SIZZLE SIZZLE

COOKED FOOD!

What Happens
Your food will cook, but it can take many hours.

Why
• Your hot dog oven is a solar collector. Sunlight hits the reflective foil surface. It focuses on the hot dog held in the center.

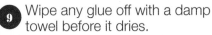

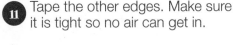

Steel Wool Wonder

34

After the washing up...
I have just the
scientific experiment
for you, my friend!

A chemical reaction is where one type of substance is chemically changed to another substance. The Sun is one big chemical reaction. The fire in your fireplace is another type of chemical reaction. Can you make another?

You will need:

thermometer, clean jar with lid, steel wool scouring pad with no soap inside, pencil, paper, bowl, vinegar

What to do in this temperature experiment

1 Put the thermometer in the jar. Put the lid on.

2 Wait about 5 minutes and write down the temperature.

3 Take the thermometer out of the jar.

4 Put a clean steel wool scouring pad in a small bowl.

5 Pour vinegar over the pad until it is completely covered. Soak it for 1 minute.

6 Lift out the steel wool and squeeze out the vinegar.

7 Wrap the steel wool around the bulb of the thermometer.

8 Place the thermometer and steel wool back in the jar. Put the lid on.

9 Wait 5 minutes, then look at the temperature. Will it be up or down?

What Happens

The temperature rises.

Why

- The vinegar takes away any protective coating from the steel wool.
- This causes the iron in the steel to rust.
- Rusting is a slow mix of iron with oxygen.
- When this chemical reaction happens, heat energy is released.
- The heat released by the rusting of the iron makes the mercury in the thermometer expand and rise.

Fun Fact

One ton of iron turns into three tons of rust. This is why the battle to stop rust forming on cars, bridges, and buildings is never-ending!

It's a true bargain! It might look like 3 tons of rust.... But there's actually 1 ton of car under that!

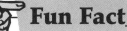

Mini Quiz

Why do some metals rust and others don't?

Mini Answer

Rust forms only on metals that have iron. It is the result of a chemical reaction between the iron and the moisture and oxygen in the air. Keeping oxygen and moisture from the surface of metal can stop rust.

35 Make a Thermometer

Rat's Rating

"The things a rat will do for science...!"

This one is to see how a thermometer works — just for fun.

You will need:

clear medicine bottle or very small jar, clear drinking straw or medicine dropper tube, cold water, spoon, food coloring, modeling clay/plasticine, marker, note book paper

What to do for this temperature experiment

1 Pour cold water into the medicine bottle. Fill to about ¼ full.

2 Add a couple of drops of food coloring.

3 Get a wad of modeling clay. Push the straw through it. Unclog the straw if bits of clay end up in it.

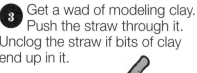

4 Put the straw in the bottle. Make sure it doesn't touch the bottom.

5 Work the modeling clay to seal the neck of the bottle. The straw needs to stay in place.

6 Blow gently into the straw so the water rises. When it is halfway up the straw, stop blowing.

7 Use your marker to make a line where the water has risen on the straw.

8 Write down the height of the water in the straw. This will be the height at room temperature.

9 Hold your hands on the bottle. Watch what happens to the height of the mixture in the bottle.

10 Mark the new level with a different color pen.

What Happens

The height of the mixture rises.

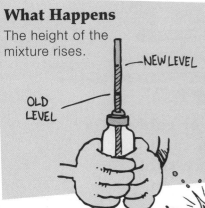

NEW LEVEL

OLD LEVEL

Why

- Just like any thermometer, the mixture expands when it becomes warm. This means the liquid no longer fits in the bottom of the bottle.
- As the water expands, the colored mixture moves up through the straw.

Fun Fact

The Italian physicist Galileo invented the first thermometer in 1593.

Mama-Mia it's-a hot in-a here! I should invent-a a THERMOMETER to see-a how hot it is! It's-a like living in-a the tropics!

Mini Quiz ?

How is temperature measured?

Mini Answer ✓

Temperature is measured on the Fahrenheit scale in the United States and in the Celsius scale in the rest of the world.

The Drip

36

Now that's some mighty speedy HOT WATER!

A puddle of sleepy slow COLD WATER

A superfast puddle of steaming HOT WATER

ZZZzzzoooooommmm

Which runs faster—hot or cold water?
Hot runs faster because you can't catch a hot, but you can catch a cold!

You will need:
2 paper cups, pins, 2 small drinking glasses, water, ice-cubes

What to do in this temperature experiment

1 In the middle of the bottom of 2 paper cups, make a tiny pinhole. Make sure they are the same size.

2 Stand the paper cups on top of the glasses.

3 Pour very cold water into 1 glass until it's ½ full.

4 Add a few ice-cubes to make sure it is really cold.

5 Pour hot water into the other glass until it is also ½ full. Watch as water drips from the paper cups into the glasses. Do you see any differences?

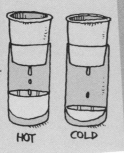

What Happens

If the holes are the same size, you'll see that the hot water leaks faster than the cold water. If the cold water is cold enough, it may not leak at all.

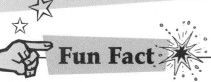

HOT   COLD

Why

- Molecules exist although we can't see them.
- The molecules in hot water move faster than in cold water.
- The faster they move, the easier it is for them to slip past each other. That is why hot water is more likely to leak than cold.

Fun Fact

You can see molecules with the help of food coloring. Get 2 drinking glasses that are exactly the same. Put ½ a cup of water in each of them. One glass should have cold tap water and the other hot tap water. Put 2 drops of food coloring in each glass. Time how long it takes for each of the colors to spread in the water. Molecules make the colors spread.

Mini Quiz

What do molecules look like?

Mini Answer ✓

Molecules are so small that it is almost impossible to see them, even with a powerful microscope. But scientists know how to make models of molecules. The models help scientists study how molecules interact.

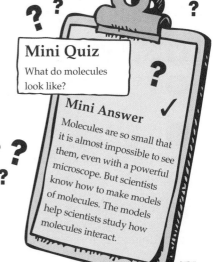

37 Pop Goes the Popcorn

Rat's Rating

O.K.! All I need now is a fizzy drink and a movie... to make this experiment complete!

Why does popcorn pop? Grab an adult to help you find out. This experiment is hot!

You will need:

unpopped popcorn, a medium pan with a clear lid, at least enough popcorn to cover the bottom of the pan, one kernel deep, ⅓ cup of oil for every cup of kernels (don't use butter), stove

What to do in this temperature experiment

1 Put the oil into the pan.

2 Place the pan on the stove.

3 Ask an adult to heat the oil so that it is very hot (if the oil smokes, it is too hot).

4 Test the oil on a couple of kernels. When they pop, add the rest of the corn.

5 Ask an adult to cover the pan and shake it so the oil spreads evenly.

6 Watch the shape and size of the corn kernels as they are heated.

7 When the popping begins to slow, ask an adult to take the pan away from the stovetop. The heated oil will still pop the rest of the kernels.

What Happens

The corn kernels change from small, hard, orange kernels to big, soft, white shapes.

Why

- The tough outside of the unpopped kernel is the *pericarp*. This is the part that often gets stuck between your teeth when you eat popcorn.
- The inside is full of starch. This grows into the white fluffy popcorn.
- The small amount of water inside the kernel makes this happen. As the kernel is heated, the water evaporates. It changes to a gas. The gas grows and pushes hard on the pericarp. It breaks and the starch tissue inside is blown outward.
- The popping noise is the sound of steam escaping and the pericarp breaking.

Fun Fact

The largest box of popcorn in the world was made in London in 2000. The box was 6 x 6 x 12 feet (1.8 x 1.8 x 3.6 meters) and filled with 784 square feet (22.2 square meters) of popcorn. It took 5 hours to fill.

I DON'T CARE WHETHER IT'S A WORLD RECORD OR NOT... It's going to AVALANCHE!

WORLD POPCORN RECORD

Mini Quiz

How did Ancient civilizations make popping corn pop?

Mini Answer ✓

In Peru, popcorn poppers date back to 300 A.D! The poppers were shallow vessels with a hole on the top and a single handle.

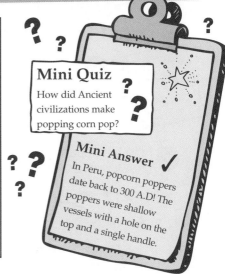

38

Too Twisty, Too Twirly

Rat's Rating

THIS MUST PROVE SOMETHING

How much power do you have in your hot little hands? Find out.

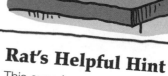

You will need:
adult supervision, thin sheet of paper, pin, pencil with eraser

Rat's Helpful Hint
This experiment works best if your hands are warm and the paper you use is light and very thin.

What to do in this temperature experiment

1 Cut your thin paper into a 3 x 3 inches (7.5 x 7.5 cm) squares.

3 Fold the square diagonally the other way.

2 Fold the square diagonally one way and then unfold it.

4 Push in gently on opposite sides of the paper. This makes the center rise about ½ inch (1.25 cm) higher than the sides.

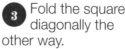

5 Push the straight pin into the eraser end of the pencil. Leave 1 inch (2.5 cm) of the pin sticking straight up.

6 Sit down and hold the pencil between your knees.

7 Set the paper square on top of the pencil. You must have the head of the pin right at the center peak where the two folds come together.

8 Cup your hands on each side of the paper. They must be about 1 inch (2.5 cm) away from it.

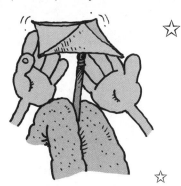

9 Do not move your hands or knees. Wait a minute and watch what happens to the paper.

What Happens
Your paper twirler will begin to turn. Once it gets going, your twirler will twirl around and around.

Why
- The warmth from your hands heats the air around them.
- The heated air rises.
- The rising air makes the finely balanced twirler twirl.

Fun Fact

Hot-air balloons don't fly in the rain. This is because balloon heat can cause water to boil on top of the balloon, and boiling water destroys the canopy fabric.

I bet nobody thought to pack an umbrella?

ROUND the WORLD ADVENTURE

Mini Quiz
What is your normal body temperature?

Mini Answer
Your normal body temperature is 98.6 degrees Fahrenheit (37 degrees Celsius). If the thermometer shows higher than this, it means you have a fever.

It's Raining Cats and Dogs

(39)

Rat's Rating

Fed up with having to water the potted plants? Bring them inside while you do this experiment. You're going to make it rain in your kitchen.

I thought the term 'RAINING CATS AND DOGS' was only just that ...a term!

WOOF

MEOW

mee-oww

AAHRRR-RUFF

You will need:
saucepan, water, ice-cubes, tray, potholder/oven mitt, an adult's supervision

What to do in this meteorology experiment

1 Put water in the saucepan.

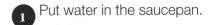

2 Ask an adult to boil the water until steam rises.

3 Hold a tray of ice-cubes above the steam. Use potholders to protect your hands.

4 Keep holding the tray until drops form on the bottom.

What Happens

The drops of water grow heavy and fall like rain.

Why

- The cold surface of the ice-cube tray cools the steam from the boiling water.
- The steam changes back into water, and collects in drops.
- As the drops get bigger and heavier, it rains.
- The boiling water is like the water that evaporates into the air as water vapor.
- As the vapor rises, it cools. You see clouds when droplets form. As these droplets collect more moisture, they become heavy enough to fall to Earth as rain.

Fun Fact

If you hold a piece of cardboard outside when it starts to rain, you can measure the size of a raindrop. A downpour has about 113 drops.

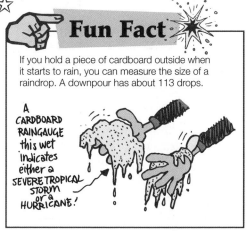

A CARDBOARD RAINGAUGE this wet indicates either a SEVERE TROPICAL STORM or a HURRICANE!

Mini Quiz

Which is the wettest place in the world? And don't answer, "In the water."

Mini Answer ✓

Mount Waialeale in Kauai, Hawaii, has the highest annual rainfall of 460 inches (1,150 cm).

40 Thirty Second Cloud

Clouds are made when air holding vaporized water cools. Try to make your own cloud inside a jar!

My...! Now that was a quick shower!

You will need:

large jar with lid, water, white chalk, zip-lock plastic bag, round balloon, scissors, thick rubber band

What to do in this meteorology experiment

1 Pour a little water into the jar. Put the lid on tightly. Leave it for 20 minutes.

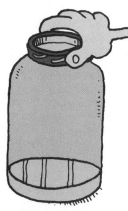

2 Put white chalk in a zip-lock bag. Zip the bag shut.

3 Use your hands to crush the chalk into a powder.

4 Cut off the neck of the balloon.

5 Take off the lid of the jar. Put in the chalk powder.

6 Quickly cover the jar with the balloon.

RUBBER BAND

8 Press the balloon down with your fist to crush the air. Hold it like this for 30 seconds.

9 Take away the balloon. What do you see?

7 Put a rubber band around the neck of the jar to keep the balloon stretched tight.

What Happens

You have made a cloud.

Why

- Cool air can't hold much water vapor. Some of it condenses to make clouds.
- When you compress the air in your jar, the air becomes warmer. It absorbs more vaporized water.
- When you take away the balloon cover, the air cools. Some of the vaporized water condenses on the chalk dust. It makes a cloud.

Fun Fact

Here are the main four groups of clouds and their shapes: cumulus (heap), stratus (layer), cirrus (curl of hair) and nimbus (rain).

A CUMULUS cloud   A STRATUS cloud

A CIRRUS cloud   A NIMBUS cloud

A rather disagreeable cranky storm cloud!

Mini Quiz

Where does the expression "on cloud nine" come from?

Mini Answer ✓

Being "on cloud nine" means you are very happy. A famous Italian author, Dante, wrote a book about ten steps to heaven. Clouds were used as the steps. Cloud nine was as close to God as you could get.

41 Heat That Rubber!

Rat's Rating

Most materials expand when heated, but some are a little different. Turn a hair dryer on a rubber band and watch what happens.

You will need:
a large rubber band, hair dryer, small light toy such as a plastic action figure, hook or doorknob on which to hang the rubber band, small table

What to do in this heat experiment

1 Attach the toy to one end of the rubber band.

2 Hang the rubber band on the hook or knob so that the toy is hanging down.

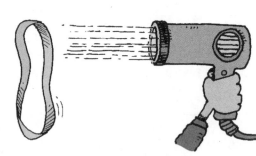

3 Place the table underneath the toy so it is just touching the table.

4 Using the hair dryer, heat the rubber band until it is very warm (this won't take long, so be careful not to melt the rubber band).

5 What is happening to the toy as you heat the rubber band?

What Happens

- As you heat the rubber band, the plastic toy is lifted off the table.
- As the rubber cools again after heating, the toy will be lowered back onto the table.

Why

- Unlike most materials, rubber shrinks when it is heated.
- Rubber molecules move around more when they are heated, and become tangled.

 **Fun Fact**

There are two types of rubber used in the world today.

Natural rubber comes from a liquid called latex, which is harvested from special rubber trees. Synthetic rubber is made from chemicals, many of which come from fossil fuels such as oil and coal.

Mini Quiz

Where do rubber trees grow?

Mini Answer

Rubber trees grow in tropical climates. The first rubber tree plantations were in South America. Today, most rubber trees are grown in South East Asia. Rubber latex is harvested from the trees by making small cuts in their trunks and allowing the sap (which contains latex) to trickle out. This is called "rubber tapping."

Stars in Your Eyes

42. It's Just a Phase

Rat's Rating

I wonder if it is made out of green cheese... ...yum! Makes your mouth water!

Ever been told, "You're just going through a phase?" Well, the moon goes through a phase, too. But it won't grow out of it.

You will need:

2 inch (5 cm) or bigger white Styrofoam ball, lamp with a bright bulb (400 watts), sharp pencil

Rat's Helpful Hint

Make sure no one's head gets in the way of this experiment, or they will cause a lunar eclipse!

What to do in this astronomy experiment

1 Put the lamp in the center of the room.

2 Take away the lampshade. You only need to see the bulb.

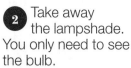

3 Push the foam ball into the sharp end of the pencil.

4 Hold the pencil in your left hand.

5 Place the ball at arm's length between the bulb and your eyes. The bulb is the Sun. The ball is the Moon. You are the Earth!

THE MOON

THE EARTH

THE S(

88

6 Your ball (Moon) is blocking the bulb (Sun). This is what a total solar eclipse looks like!

7 Move your ball (Moon) so that you look into the bulb (Sun). Look at your moon. All of the light shines on the far side. This is opposite the side you are looking at. This phase is called the *new moon.*

8 Move your hand to the left, about 45 degrees of the way around counterclockwise. Look at the light on your Moon. The right hand edge is lit as a crescent. The crescent starts out very thin. It fattens up as the Moon moves farther away from the Sun.

9 When your Moon is at 90 degrees to the left, the right half of the Moon lights up.

10 Keep moving your hand counter-clockwise. When the Moon reaches directly opposite the Sun, the part seen from Earth is fully lit. Of course, only half of the Moon is lit. It has taken the Moon about 2 weeks to move from new to full.

11 Switch the pencil to your right hand. Face the lamp.

12 Start with your Moon at full. Keep going on its counterclockwise course. You'll see the opposite phases of the Moon. The Moon will reach the 270° position, straight out to the right. A thinning crescent and a return to new moon follows this.

What Happens

The Moon chases the Sun across the day and night sky.

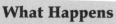

Why

- From full to new, the Moon has been waning and leading the Sun.
- The phase cycle takes 29.53 days. Why not watch the real Moon? Most newspapers give the Moon phases along with the weather data.

Meet a Meteor

Rat's Rating

WHOA! Will you look at that! A little bit of something ...from somewhere in space!

Meteors are small chunks of broken comets or asteroids. As they enter Earth's atmosphere, they burn up. Find out if this is fact or friction.

You will need:
large soda bottle, warm water, seltzer tablet

What to do in this astronomy experiment

1 Fill the bottle with warm tap water.

2 Drop the seltzer tablet into the bottle. Watch what happens.

What Happens

The seltzer tablet breaks up into many small pieces. These disappear as it travels to the bottom of the bottle.

Why

- The water is like the atmosphere of the Earth. The tablet is like the meteor.
- Like a meteor, the tablet breaks up into many small pieces as it drops to the bottom of the bottle (the surface of the Earth).
- Meteors travel through space at great speeds.
- The force of their surfaces rubs against the atmosphere of the Earth. This makes them heat up so much that they break up and explode into space dust.

Mini Quiz ?

Are there different types of friction?

Mini Answer ✓

There are two main types of friction. These are *static* and *kinetic*. Static friction is the amount of resistance to movement when an object is static, or not moving. Kinetic friction is the resistance on a moving object. Kinetic friction can be sliding or rolling friction.

Fun Fact

Every day, a thousand tons of meteor dust falls on the Earth.

AHHRRR... Meteor dust!

44 Micrometeorites

Rat's Rating

Perhaps it's a little piece of Pluto!

Has a meteor landed in your backyard?
Try this experiment. You might be surprised.

You will need:
sheet of white paper, small paint brush, jar, magnet, microscope

What to do in this astronomy experiment

1 Find a place in your house where floating bits of fine particles collect. Window and door screens and the bottom of outside drain spouts work well.

2 Use a brush to collect the particles. Make sure they are dry and put them in a small jar.

3 Shake the particles onto a sheet of white paper. Roll the sides up. Gently tap all the particles into the center of the sheet.

4 Place a magnet under the paper.

5 Gently tilt and tap the paper to get rid of non-magnetic particles. What is left?

What Happens

Some of the left-over metallic particles are bits of space dust! To look at them, place the paper under a microscope. You'll need to use high power to see them clearly. The micrometeorites will show signs of their fiery trip through the atmosphere. They will be rounded and may have small pits on their surfaces.

WOW! There's a whole METEORITE SHOWER going on here!

Why

- Tons of space dust and debris blast the Earth every day.
- Much of what you see are particles that date from when the solar system was formed.
- This is debris left from the raw materials that formed into the eight known planets and the asteroids. This was 4–5 billion years ago!
- Most particles have been broken off, or ground down from larger objects.

Fun Fact

Shooting stars are not really stars. They are small bits of rock and metal that hit into the upper atmosphere of Earth. And, because of friction, burn up. Sometimes, man-made satellites and spacecraft parts fall into the atmosphere. These burn up the same way.

Well there goes the satellite broadcast of the big match.... because there goes the satellite through the Earth's atmosphere!

Mini Quiz

Why are pieces of rock so important?

Mini Answer ✓

Meteorites are very important for scientists to study. Apart from a small amount of moon rock brought back by the *Apollo* and *Luner* missions, meteorites are the only material evidence that there is a universe beyond the Earth.

Sounds of Science

45 Straw Oboe

Rat's Rating

AHHRR... My favourite OBOE CONCERTO!

We hope that you enjoyed this live performance of the DRINKING STRAW CONCERTO in G MINOR.

It sounded like an OBOE to me!

Here is your chance to make all the noise you want— and you can blame it all on science.

You will need:
drinking straw, ☆
scissors

Rat's Helpful Hint

Try this early on a Sunday morning when the rest of the house is asleep. The best way to do it is to stand by a bedroom door. Be careful though, sound bytes bite, so maybe you really shouldn't!

What to do in this sound experiment

1 Pinch flat ½ inch to ¾ inch (12–19 mm) at one end of the straw.

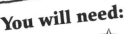

2 Cut off little triangles. These make the reeds.

3 Put the straw far enough into your mouth so your lips do not touch the corners.

4 Press ☆ with your lips on the straw, but not too hard.
Blow gently just past the cut. Listen to the sound. Keep trying. It may take a few tries.

94

5 Cut three small slits along the length of the straw about 1 inch (2.5 cm) apart.

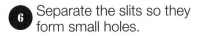

7 Cover one of them and blow as before.

6 Separate the slits so they form small holes.

8 Then cover two, then three, blowing each time. Keep listening.

What Happens

Each time you blow, you hear a different sound. You can play simple tunes by covering and uncovering the holes.

Why

- As in a real oboe, the reeds open and close at high speed.
- This first allows air to flow into the straw and then to stop the flow.
- Vibrating air makes the sound.
- As you cover and uncover the holes, you regulate the length of the air column. That decides the pitch.
- The shorter the air column, the faster it vibrates and the higher the note.

Fun Fact

Another way to be heard is with a piece of cellophane 2 inches (5 cm) square. Stretch it tightly between the thumbs and index fingers of both hands. Hold your hands in front of your face so the cellophane is in front of your lips. Blow hard and fast at the edge of the tightly stretched piece of cellophane. Keep your lips close together. You must send a thin stream of air right at the edge of the cellophane.

Can you hear a noise? When the air hits the edge of the cellophane, you'll make a scream. If you don't, change the distance between the cellophane and your lips until the air hits it just right. The fast moving air from your lip makes the edges of the cellophane vibrate. Because the cellophane is very thin, the jet of air makes these vibrations very fast. The faster something vibrates, the higher the tone it creates.

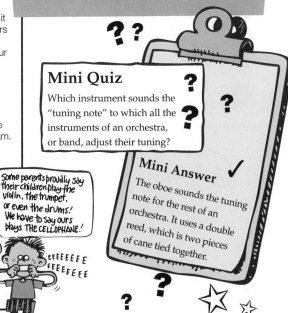

Some parents proudly say their children play the violin, the trumpet, or even the drums! We have to say ours plays THE CELLOPHANE!

Mini Quiz

Which instrument sounds the "tuning note" to which all the instruments of an orchestra, or band, adjust their tuning?

Mini Answer ✓

The oboe sounds the tuning note for the rest of an orchestra. It uses a double reed, which is two pieces of cane tied together.

Shake That Salt

46

Rat's Rating

I could swear that SALT was over there next to the pepper a second ago... ...must be part of this experiment!

Don't you hate it when no one passes you the salt at the dinner table? Let's make salt move without touching it. Is it a mystery? Is it magic? Or is it science?

What to do in this sound experiment

1 Pull the plastic tightly over the open end of the large can.

2 Put the rubber band over it.

3 Sprinkle some salt on top of the plastic.

4 Hold the small can close to the salt. Tap the side of the small can with the ruler. What do you think will happen to the salt?

What Happens

The salt moves! Tap the small can in different spots or hold it in different directions. Find out how you need to hold and tap the can to get the salt to move the most.

Why

- Sound vibrations travel through the air, and when they hit the plastic stretched over the can like a drum, it vibrates.
- This causes the salt to bounce.
- Your ear also has a drum.
- It's called an eardrum and works because of sound vibrations too.

Fun Fact

You can make even the lightest taps of your fingers sound loud. Sit at a table and place your ear flat on the tabletop. Tap with your finger on the surface of the table about 1 foot (30 cm) away from your ear. Tap hard. Then tap softly. The sound of your tapping finger is much louder than when you listen to the same tapping normally. This is because sound waves travel through solids too! Many solids like wood carry sound waves much better than air. This is because the molecules in wood are closer together than those in air.

He says it's part of a scientific experiment... ...but I think it's just an excuse to not eat his BEANS

Mini Quiz ?

How fast does sound travel?

Mini Answer ✓

Sound travels through the air at about 1,129 feet per second (344 meters). The speed of light travels about 186,000 miles per second (300,000 km). To find out how far away you are from a thunderstorm, count the seconds that pass between seeing the lightning flash and hearing the thunder. Divide the number of seconds by 5 (for miles) or by 3 (for km). So, how far away is the storm?

String Orchestra

47

Rat's Rating

As a child...I practised playing 'THE STRING'. Let's be thankful I took it no further...'

FEEEEE EEEE
eeee eeee

String instruments make sounds with vibrating strings. Let's see if you can too.

You will need:
2 pieces of string, paper cup, paperclips, small can, water

What to do in this sound experiment

1 Half fill the small can with water.

2 Tie 1 paperclip to the end of 1 piece of string.

3 Put the other string through the hole in the paper cup.

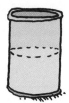

4 Tie the second paperclip to the end of the string in the paper cup.

5 Hold up the string without the cup by the paperclip.

98

6 Wet your fingertips in the can of water.

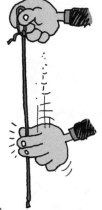

7 Squeeze the string between your fingertips near the paperclip. Pull your fingers down the string. You should hear a sound.

8 Hold up the cup with the string hanging down.

☆

9 Get your fingers wet again.

☆

10 Squeeze the string and pull your fingers down it. You should hear another sound. What is different about the two sounds?

☆ ☆

Why

- Vibrations in the string make the cup vibrate too.
- Since the cup is bigger, it moves more air. This makes a louder sound.
- The same thing happens with instruments like the violin. The vibrating strings make the wood body vibrate. This makes a louder sound.

What Happens

The sound from the cup is louder.

Fun Fact

The vibrating parts of musical instruments don't make sound waves of just one frequency. This is because the string, or forced air, doesn't just vibrate as a whole. Smaller parts also vibrate. In musical instruments, the extra frequencies are called *overtones*. When the overtones are close to the basic frequency, your brain thinks it's a single pitch (level of sound). Different instruments have different strengths of their overtones. This is also what makes your voice sound different from someone else's, even when you sing the exact same pitch.

Mini Quiz

How do you measure sound?

? ? ?

Mini Answer ✓

Sound is measured in decibels (dB)—this is the force of sound waves against the ear. The louder the sound, the more decibels it is. Here are approximate decibel levels for some everyday sounds:

Watch ticking 20
Normal talking 50
Doorbell 80
Baby crying 110
Sporting event 120
Kid's noisy squeeze toy 135
Rock concert 140
Jet engine taking off 150
Fireworks 160
Shotgun fire 170
Rocket launch 180.

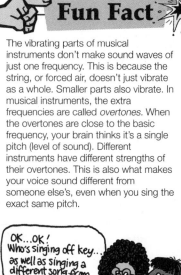

OK...OK! Who's singing off key... as well as singing a different song from everyone else?

It's a Pushover

Be a Conductor

Rat's Rating

My faithful old rubber sandal. Are you a CONDUCTOR or an INSULATOR? That is the question!

Does electricity go through everything? Find out.

Rat's Helpful Hint

If you're barefooted, don't step on any electric wires. You might get a pair of shocks!

You will need:

spring type clothespin, 1 D-cell battery, aluminum foil or 2 plastic-covered copper wires, flashlight bulb, masking tape, scissors, ruler, materials to test: safety pin, coins, cork, rubber band, leaf, water, paperclip, glass, plastic

What to do in this electricity experiment

1 If using copper wires, skip to step number 5.

2 Cut the foil into a rectangle 24 in. x 12 in. (60 cm x 30 cm).

3 Fold the foil in half along its length. Do this 5 times to make a thin strip 24 in. (60 cm) long.

FOLD FOIL TO MAKE ONE STRIP

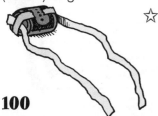

4 Cut the foil strip in half to make two 24 in. (60 cm) strips.

5 Tape one end of both strips to the ends of the battery.

6 Wrap the other end of one strip around the base of the flashlight bulb. Fix the clothespin around the strip on the end of the lightbulb.

7 Test your materials to see if they conduct electricity. Touch the metal tip on the bottom of the flashlight bulb to one side of the material. At the same time, touch the free end of the metal strip to the opposite side of the same material.

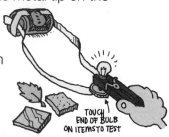

TOUCH END OF BULB ON ITEMS TO TEST

What Happens

Some of your materials will let electricity flow through them and light the bulb. These materials are called *conductors*. Any living thing such as plants, animals, and trees are good conductors as well as wire, metal, and water. An *insulator* is a material that electricity doesn't easily flow through. Items such as plastic, rubber, and glass are good insulators.

Why

- An electric circuit is the path through which electrons move.
- A switch is a material that acts as a bridge for the electrons.
- When the circuit is closed by a switch, the electrons do not move freely.
- When it is open, the electrons move along the circuit.
- When you touch a good conductor and the tip of the bulb to the other side, you open a circuit.
- The electrons flow from the negative part of the battery through the foil conductor and into the bulb.
- The electrons go from the bulb through the foil and back into the positive end of the battery.
- As long as there is no break in the system, the electrons keep flowing and the bulb stays lit.

☞ Fun Fact

Electricity is measured in units of power called *watts*. It was named after James Watt, the inventor of the steam engine. One watt is a very small amount of power. It takes nearly 750 watts to equal 1 horsepower. A kilowatt equals 1,000 watts. The waste made by one chicken in its lifetime can supply enough electricity to run a 100 watt bulb for five hours!

So what are you calling your new unit to measure electricity sir?

WATT

I said what are you calling the new unit to measure electricity?

WATT

Forget it... we're getting nowhere here... I'll wait until I get my first power bill.

Mini Quiz

Why must you never swim or play outdoors during a thunderstorm? **?**

Mini Answer ✓

Lightning is a natural form of electricity. You are a good conductor of electricity. Being struck by lightning would kill you.

49 Iron for Breakfast

Rat's Rating

Feeling hungry? Would you eat an iron nail? Most enriched breakfast cereals add metallic iron as a health supplement. Try this experiment.

You will need:

2 different breakfast cereals (one healthy, one not!), bowls, pencil, magnets, zip-lock plastic bags, tape, water, white coffee filter papers/paper towels, microscope or magnifying glass

What to do in this chemistry experiment

1 Put ½ cup of each cereal into 2 separate zip-lock bags. Zip up the bags.

2 Use your hands to crush the cereal to a fine powder.

3 Pour each crushed cereal into a different bowl.

4 Add 1 cup of water to each bowl and stir. If needed, use extra water to keep the mixture thin and soupy.

6 Stir the cereal mix with the magnet for 10 minutes.

5 Tape a small magnet to the eraser end of a pencil. Seal it inside a plastic bag.

7 Lift out the magnet. What do you see? Gently wipe the magnet on the filter paper.

What Happens

Small bits of pure iron filings have collected on the magnet! The filings will look like small dark dots on the magnet. Sometimes, they'll clump together. If you have trouble seeing the filings, try looking through a microscope or magnifying glass.

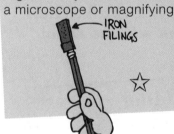

IRON FILINGS

Why

- Magnets attract iron.
- Magnets will stick to anything that has iron in it.
- Our bodies don't have very much iron, so magnets don't stick to us.

Fun Fact ☆

The human body needs iron for many functions. Most importantly, iron is used to make *hemoglobin* in red blood cells. It is the iron in the hemoglobin that attracts oxygen molecules. This lets the blood cells carry oxygen to other cells in the body. Red blood cells are always being replaced. This is why your diet needs a constant supply of iron. Iron is put in some foods and vitamin pills as a healthy additive.

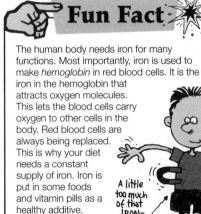

A little too much of that IRON-enriched breakfast cereal

Mini Quiz ?

Is the iron in cereals the same iron as found in nails, cars, and machinery?

Mini Answer ✓

Yes! The iron in cereal is pure iron! Really! It's mixed in the cereal batter along with other additives. The tiny particles of iron quickly react with hydrochloric acid and other chemicals in the digestive tract. This changes them into a form easily absorbed by the body.

50 Am I Attractive?

Rat's Rating

OK! I'm lost! I'm a SCIENTIST, not an explorer!

Magnets are more human than you think. Their poles can attract each other as well as repel each other.

You will need:
modeling clay, sharp pencil with an eraser, horseshoe magnet

Rat's Helpful Hint
Just remember to keep your magnet away from audio and videotapes and computer disks, or you might erase the information on them!

What to do in this magnets experiment

1 Roll the piece of clay into a ball.

2 Flatten it to make a cone shape.

3 Push the eraser end of the pencil into the clay.

4 Carefully balance the horseshoe magnet on the pencil lead.

What Happens
The magnet slowly moves itself into a north–south direction.

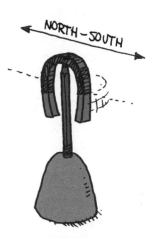

NORTH – SOUTH

Why

- The Earth has a magnetic field, which isn't very strong, but it's enough to attract your magnet. The magnet turned in a north–south direction.
- Five billion years ago, the Earth was made in a big mix of meteorites and comets. The huge amount of heat melted the planet. It's still cooling off today!
- Denser materials like iron from the meteorites sank to create the core of the Earth. As it rotated, it made a magnetic field.

Fun Fact

Cows like to graze on grass. Unfortunately, bolts, nails, and bits of barbed wire end up in the grass. The cows eat these by mistake. Some cows have even died when trying to pass them through their digestive system. To solve the problem, farmers can feed calves magnets! The magnets stay in the cow's stomachs their whole life and hold onto the metal. This means the metal doesn't go through their digestive systems.

Mini Quiz

Imagine that you are in the middle of the ocean. All you see is water and it is a cloudy day so you cannot see the sun. How would you know which way to go?

Mini Answer ✓

No matter where you are on Earth, you can hold a compass and it will point toward the North Pole. Long before space satellites and other high-tech navigational aids, a compass was the best way to know which way to go.

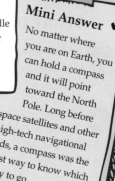

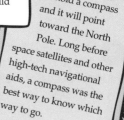

She calls it 'a magnetic personality.' But I think there's something else going on there!

51 # Balloon Lung

Rat's Rating

What does your lung look like when it breathes air? Find out!

Another Birthday Party! That means BALLOON LUNG!

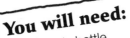

You will need:

clear plastic bottle,
balloon,
plastic funnel

Rat's Helpful Hint

Make sure the bottle has your favorite drink. That way you'll get a chance to drink it all before you start the experiment.

What to do in this anatomy experiment

1 Blow up and let out the air in a balloon 10 times. This makes it soft and baggy.

2 Push the balloon ½ inch (1 cm) over the neck of a funnel about 5 inches (14 cm) wide.

COOL SCIENCE EXPERIMENTS

3 Push the balloon and neck of the funnel into a clear plastic bottle. The balloon should partly inflate.

4 Squeeze the sides of the bottle and let go of your grip 10 times. What does the balloon do?

breathe out

What Happens
The balloon is breathing just like a real lung.

breathe in

Why
- The air is forced out of the balloon.
- When you release your grip, the balloon fills again.
- When you breathe in, the muscles in your chest cavity contract and expand.
- This makes the pressure in the chest cavity lower than the outside air pressure.
- Air then flows in through the airways and inflates the lungs.
- When you breathe out, your muscles relax. Your chest cavity gets smaller.
- The decrease in volume of the cavity increases the pressure in the chest cavity above the outside air pressure.
- Air from the lungs (high pressure) then flows out of the airways to the outside air (low pressure). The cycle then repeats with each breath.

Fun Fact

Forests are the "lungs" of the world as we need them for the air we breathe. To survive, a tree uses carbon dioxide and gives off oxygen. They are like oxygen factories and are essential to the survival of the planet.

What if every tree in the forest breathed out at the same time!

Mini Quiz
Which part of your body has a surface area about the same size as a tennis court?

Mini Answer
Your lungs.

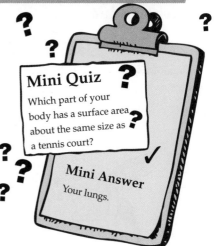

52 Floating Ball

A rat needs to have his fur looking just right for the big match!

That includes eyebrow

Can a ball float on an invisible stream of air?

You will need: ☆
a hair dryer, ping-pong ball/round balloon/Styrofoam ball, tissue

What to do in this physics experiment ☆

1 Turn on the hair dryer.

2 Blow a stream of air straight up.

3 Carefully balance the ping-pong ball above the stream of air.

4 Pull it slowly out of the stream. What do you see? When only half the ball is out of the stream of air, you can feel it being sucked back.

5 Let go of the ball. It will waver back and forth and then settle near the center of the stream of air.

☆ ☆ COOL SCIENCE EXPERIMENTS

6 Keep the ball a little way out of the stream of air. With the other hand, dangle a tissue and look for the stream of air above the ball. See how the ball turns the stream outward.

☆

7 Tilt the stream of air to one side and see how the ball is still hanging.

8 Balance the ball in the stream of air.

☆

9 Move the hair dryer and the ball toward the corner of a room. Look at how much higher the hanging ball moves.

What Happens

The ping-pong ball floats freely in the air. When you try to pull the ball out of the stream of air, you can feel a force pulling it back in. You can feel the ball turning the stream.

Why

- When the ball is hanging in the stream of air, the air flowing up hits the bottom of the ball.
- It slows and makes an area of higher pressure.
- The high pressure area of air under the ball holds the ball up against the pull of gravity.
- When you pull the ball a little bit out of the stream, the air flows around the curve of the ball that is nearest the center of the stream of air.
- Air rushes in an arc around the top of the ball. It then moves out above the ball.
- This outward flowing air puts out an inward force on the ball.

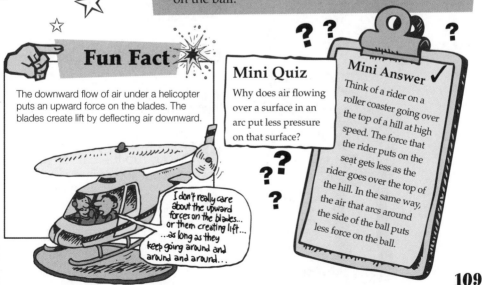

Fun Fact

The downward flow of air under a helicopter puts an upward force on the blades. The blades create lift by deflecting air downward.

I don't really care about the upward forces on the blades... ...or them creating lift... ...as long as they keep going around and around and around...

Mini Quiz

Why does air flowing over a surface in an arc put less pressure on that surface?

Mini Answer ✓

Think of a rider on a roller coaster going over the top of a hill at high speed. The force that the rider puts on the seat gets less as the rider goes over the top of the hill. In the same way, the air that arcs around the side of the ball puts less force on the ball.

Glow Balloon

53

What happens when a balloon meets a fluorescent light?

GLOW BALLOONS... ...spooky!

You will need:
balloon, fluorescent light tube

What to do in this electricity experiment

1 Blow up the balloon. Seal it off.

2 Wash the outside of the fluorescent tube. Dry it well.

3 In a dark room, place one end of the tube against the floor.

4 Hold the tube upright. Quickly rub the balloon up and down the outside of it.

5 Hold the balloon near the tube.

What Happens

The fluorescent tube starts to glow. The light moves with the movement of the balloon. Once the tube starts glowing, even the nearness of the balloon makes light.

Why

- A fluorescent light has tiny threads at each end. When the chemicals on the threads meet with an electrical current, they make electricity.
- The electricity jumps from one end of the light to the other. It makes 120 flashes of light every second.
- Inside a fluorescent light is mercury vapor.
- The mercury vapor gives out ultraviolet light when an electric current passes through it.
- Your eyes don't see ultraviolet light. So, the inside of a fluorescent tube is coated with a phosphor. This coating changes the ultraviolet energy into light energy that you can see. We say the phosphor fluoresces.
- When you rub the balloon on the light, you make the same changes, but in a smaller way.
- Rubbing the balloon makes electrons build up on the balloon.
- This charges the mercury vapor inside the tube the same way electricity does.
- The charged mercury vapor gives off ultraviolet light. This makes the fluorescent chemicals inside the tube also give off light.

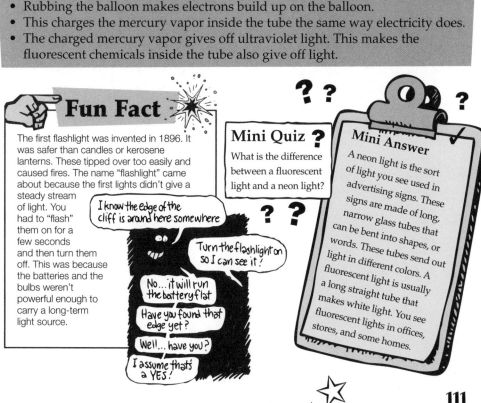

Fun Fact

The first flashlight was invented in 1896. It was safer than candles or kerosene lanterns. These tipped over too easily and caused fires. The name "flashlight" came about because the first lights didn't give a steady stream of light. You had to "flash" them on for a few seconds and then turn them off. This was because the batteries and the bulbs weren't powerful enough to carry a long-term light source.

I know the edge of the cliff is around here somewhere

Turn the flashlight on so I can see it!

No... it will run the battery flat

Have you found that edge yet?

Well... have you?

I assume that's a YES!

Mini Quiz ?

What is the difference between a fluorescent light and a neon light?

Mini Answer

A neon light is the sort of light you see used in advertising signs. These signs are made of long, narrow glass tubes that can be bent into shapes, or words. These tubes send out light in different colors. A fluorescent light is usually a long straight tube that makes white light. You see fluorescent lights in offices, stores, and some homes.